HERE
WE
STAND

JOSEPH FIELDING McCONKIE

DESERET BOOK COMPANY · SALT LAKE CITY, UTAH

Library of Congress Cataloging-in-Publication Data

McConkie, Joseph F.
    Here we stand / Joseph Fielding McConkie.
        p.   cm.
    Includes bibliographical references and index.
    ISBN 1-57345-045-6 (hdbk.)
    1. Mormon Church—Apologetic works. 2. Mormon Church—Doctrines.
I. Title.
BX8635.5.M329   1995
230'.9332—dc20   95-258
                                                    CIP

Printed in the United States of America

10 9 8 7 6 5 4 3 2 1

*That the church may stand independent
above all other creatures beneath the celestial world.*
—*Doctrine and Covenants 78:14*

CONTENTS

INTRODUCTION

IF THERE IS A GOD IN heaven and if we are his children, as holy writ attests, then he must have a plan for our salvation, for surely the purpose of our creation must reach beyond the experiences of this mortal state. And if indeed he has a plan for our salvation, it must follow as the night the day that those entrusted with that saving knowledge receive it with the sacred covenant that they will share it with all who will listen. Again, we would reason that if there be but one God, there can be but one plan of salvation and that all his children have equal claim upon its blessings. Surely no church could profess to be his Church without at the same time professing the responsibility to take the gospel given them to those of every nation, kindred, tongue, and people.

As members of The Church of Jesus Christ of Latter-day Saints, we have been entrusted with the message of salvation and the commission to take that message to the ends of the earth. To do so, we must have a clear and certain understanding of what we are to teach. We cannot teach what we do not know, any more than we can come back from where we have not been. Ours is the message of the Restoration. It is founded on the testimony that the Father and the Son appeared to the youthful Joseph Smith in a grove, now called sacred, in the spring of 1820. That event signaled the beginning of a great gospel dispensation, one destined to embrace the restoration of the gospel of Jesus Christ in its pristine purity once again to the earth. That restored gospel is our message.

The rock upon which the latter-day Church of Jesus Christ rests is not the revelation of Christ to Peter or to the meridian Twelve. It is the revelation of Christ to the Prophet Joseph Smith in the Sacred Grove coupled with the revelation of Christ to each individual member. We are not borrowing the testimony of the ancients. We stand independent. Our testimony is immediate and personal. It is of a God who lives and manifests himself to the pure in heart in this day as he did in ages past. We glory in the testimony of prophets of ages past, but we do not seek salvation in the promises made to others. We know God other than by hearsay. The house of our understanding is fashioned like that of the Saints of earlier ages, but the stones of our faith are of our own cutting: like them we have living prophets, and like them we have a God who speaks.

We part paths with historical Christianity in that we believe that shortly after the death of Christ and his apostles, there was a universal apostasy, or corrupting of the doctrines of Christ, and a subsequent loss of the authority to minister in his name. Just as there is no salvation in the worship of a false Christ, so there can be no salvation in corrupted doctrines or false priesthoods. If it can successfully be argued otherwise, there is no need for the real Jesus or pure doctrines. If salvation can be had independent of Christ or by the acceptance of false notions of him or his doctrines, then his ministry and word are without purpose. We exist as his Church because we believe that a true knowledge of Christ, the purity of his doctrines, and the authority to act in his name were restored to the earth through the instrumentality of the Prophet Joseph Smith.

In the context of missionary work, or the labor of sharing the restored gospel, if someone were to say to us, "I accept your message and believe what you are teaching to be true except the part about Christ," we could only conclude that he had missed the heart and soul of our message. In the gospel cause, to believe the right things for the wrong reasons or even to do right things for the wrong reasons—whatever those reasons might be—is to cast the seeds of faith by the wayside where they can neither obtain depth of root nor produce good fruits. Again, if someone were to say, "I can accept everything you teach except the part about Joseph Smith," we would know that he had not understood the message we have been commissioned to teach. We could hardly imagine someone claiming to have embraced Judaism while rejecting "the part about Moses." To embrace the law of Moses, in any meaningful way, certainly requires the acceptance of Moses as the Lord's prophet and the covenant spokesman. Were it not for Moses, there could be no law of Moses. That, however, does not justify confusing the messenger with the message. Ancient Israel did not expect to find salvation in Moses, nor do they today. They did, however, expect to be blessed by obedience to the law, or covenant, that Moses brought in the name, or authority, of God. To reject Moses would be to reject that authority. As with Moses, so with Joseph Smith. We cannot reject him and profess to accept the message he brought. He stands at the head of the greatest of all gospel dispensations, and every valid testimony must be founded on the witness of the Spirit that Joseph Smith is the revelator of Christ for all that live in this dispensation and that he is the conduit of restored authority for every ordinance of salvation that is performed.

This truth is simple enough to illustrate. Every priesthood holder should be able to trace his priesthood back to Christ himself. In this dispensation no one can do so without going through Joseph Smith. To be of "efficacy, virtue, or force" in this world or the next, all ordinances must be performed by authority restored to Joseph Smith and under the direction of keys given to him. Every doctrine and ordinance of salvation that we profess as a Church traces itself to the Prophet Joseph Smith. Simply stated, he links us to Christ. We do not baptize in the name of Joseph Smith, or administer the sacrament in his name, or pray to him or any other supposed saint. Our faith is in Christ, and Joseph Smith is his great witness and spokesman for this dispensation. Just as you cannot talk about the events of Sinai without talking about Moses, so we cannot testify of the restored gospel without testifying of the divine role played by Joseph Smith.

In sharing our message, we find those who fear that if we mention Joseph Smith, we will be accused of worshiping him rather than Christ. Two observations ought to be made in response to such feelings. First, any response that is born of fear is devoid of the Spirit. Second, we can hardly profess to be on the Lord's errand, to be his messengers, if we let the adversary dictate our agenda. If someone can find a doctrine that does not make the minions of hell protest, then he has found a doctrine that does not matter. A doctrine that Satan does not seek to distort and attack is hardly worth preaching. Those that he rants the most about are obviously those he fears the most and thus the ones we ought to be preaching the most.

If we attempt to hide every doctrine that our critics distort, we are going to be left speechless. It is as if we revel in the fruits of the gospel but are ashamed of the tree from which they come. That notion reminds me of a woman I met in Jerusalem some years ago. She professed a belief in the prophets of the Old Testament while proclaiming herself an atheist. Somehow it never dawned on her that there isn't any reason to have a prophet who is supposed to be God's spokesman if there is no God. What she was really saying was that she was angry with God for the Holocaust and so had rejected him. The ancient prophets were not responsible for her suffering, and so she continued to reverence them. Hers was a contorted form of reasoning, but no more so than those who attempt to dissociate the fruits of the restored gospel from the reality of the First Vision or the role of the Prophet who stands at its head.

It is fashionable among many attempting to share our message to first seek common ground with those they desire to teach. That is a rather strange notion. Can you imagine a salesman attempting to convince you that his product is just like the one you are using? If he is right, why in the world would you want to change? I witnessed a perfect illustration of this approach in a priesthood meeting in a small branch. The missionaries had an investigator present. He was a very intelligent and fine man who was active in the Catholic faith. During the meeting the branch members did everything they could think of to convince this man that we, as Latter-day Saints, were just like him. They succeeded. At the end of the meeting he got up, walked out the door, and never came back. He told the missionaries on the way out he could see no reason to leave an established church to join one that was trying so hard to be just like what he already had.

Our inconsistencies may be more apparent to others than they are to us. A letter recently addressed to the editor of a Utah Valley newspaper by a local pastor illustrates this point. Bearing the title "On Common Ground," it chided Latter-day Saints for not knowing where they stood. "Most Mormons I meet," the minister wrote, "seem to be looking for common ground with the Christian community at large. Mormonism then relates to the outside world in two ways. On the one hand, there is the desire for acceptance, the desire to be able to say, 'We are Christians too.' [The not-too-subtle implication here is that Mormons are not Christians.] On the other hand, there is the actual theology of Mormonism that grows out of the idea of the

Apostasy and the belief that the LDS Church is the restoration of Christ's one true Church. This theology motivates the missionary movement of the LDS Church, which seeks to win converts from churches that are a part of apostate Christianity. The two different approaches are not compatible. What I find myself asking is why the LDS Church is so intent on finding common ground with the very churches it considers to be apostate? Why does it seek acceptance from the very people it seeks to convert?"

The minister's criticism is a little embarrassing. It gives us the feeling that we have been caught. Certainly we want to avoid giving offense and of course we want to be accepted as Christians, but at what cost? Should we trade our birthright to be thought acceptable by a corrupted form of Christianity? And what becomes of our faith if we embrace the notion that we are sharing common ground with the churches of the world? In religion classes that I teach at Brigham Young University I have found with some consistency that if I say, "We are members of the only true and living Church on the face of the earth," not even a ripple passes through the classroom. If, on the other hand, I say, "We believe all other churches to be false," I can expect someone to take offense at my intemperate and intolerant expression. It is as if we thought we could stand for something without being against anything. It is as if we could pick up one side of a stick while leaving the other undisturbed.

The message of the Restoration centers on the idea that it is not common ground we seek in sharing the gospel. There is nothing common about our message. The way we answer questions about our faith ought to be by finding the quickest and most direct route to the Sacred Grove. That is our ground. It is sacred ground. It is where the heavens are opened and the God of heaven speaks. It is where testimonies are born and the greatest truths of heaven are unveiled. It is of this sacred ground that we say, *here we stand.*

Chapter One

A SURE FOUNDATION

Remember that it is upon the rock of our Redeemer, who is Christ, the Son of God, that ye must build your foundation; that when the devil shall send forth his mighty winds, yea, his shafts in the whirlwind, yea, when all his hail and his mighty storm shall beat upon you, it shall have no power over you to drag you down to the gulf of misery and endless wo, because of the rock upon which ye are built, which is a sure foundation, a foundation whereon if men build they cannot fall.
—Helaman 5:12

THE CHRISTIAN FAITH has always claimed to be in possession of a body of truth that exceeds in dignity and value all other knowledge. It responds to the most important issues of our existence. It reconciles humankind to God, teaching not only of his character and attributes but how we may commune with Deity and obtain both communal and individual revelation of his will. It explains the origin of the universe and of humanity. It answers such questions as, Where did we come from? Why do we exist on this earth? and What becomes of us at death? It is an unmatched source of peace and assurance. It gives meaning, purpose, and direction to all that we do. It embraces a saving provision, which, if properly acted upon, has the effect of establishing a filial relationship with God, of changing character, and conveying a promise of life beyond the grave in conditions of endless happiness.

BUILDING A SURE FOUNDATION

How, it ought be asked, is the Christian claim to the truths of salvation to be sustained? That is, how are we to know that God is the source of the answers that are being given in his name? I suggest there are three essential parts to the answer to this question. The first is to establish the authority of the agent through whom the message comes. Only if the agent is trustworthy should serious consideration be given to his message. Second, the message must evidence itself. That is, it must have the ring of truth. It must have a light and power of its own. Third, it must give offense where offense ought to be given. The principle here is the simple verity that we cannot do the Lord's work without offending the adversary. If there are truths that lead to salvation, then of necessity they will be opposed by falsehoods that lead to damnation.

JESUS AS THE MESSENGER OF SALVATION

In establishing his claim of being the promised Messiah, Jesus of Nazareth professed no authority from the Jews. In priesthood and doctrine he stood independent. All that he espoused professed divine revelation as its source. We are told that "he spake not as other men, neither could he be taught; for he needed not that any man should teach him" (JST Matthew 3:25). When he taught, "the Jews marveled, saying, How knoweth this man letters, having never learned?" (John

7:15), which is to say, how is it that one who has not been to our schools and trained for the ministry can have such understanding?

Matthew tells us that Jesus taught as "one having authority, and not as the scribes" (Matthew 7:29). The rabbis knew no authority save that of tradition; they could quote endlessly from those of ages past but made no pretense to priesthood or the spirit of prophecy. The Joseph Smith Translation rendering of Matthew 7:29 states that Christ taught as one "having authority from God, and not as having authority from the Scribes" (JST Matthew 7:37). Again, Jesus said, "As my Father hath taught me, I speak these things" (John 8:28). Christ had the audacity to edit and even eclipse scripture. Repeatedly, in the Sermon on the Mount, he said, "Ye have heard that it was said by them of old time," and then, having quoted something from the law of Moses, he would say, "but I say unto you" and give differing instruction (Matthew 5:21; see also vv. 22, 27, 28, 32, 34, 39, 44). In each of these instances, he was forcing a choice between the loyalty his disciples had for scripture and the loyalty they had for him as the living voice of God. Many have argued about the authority that Christ professed. Their arguments can be sustained only by denying the legitimacy of the scriptural texts that have been preserved for us. If one is paying attention, it is hard to miss the implications of such statements as "I send unto you prophets, and wise men, and scribes: and some of them ye shall kill and crucify; and some of them shall ye scourge in your synagogues, and persecute them from city to city" (Matthew 23:34). If Christ is the one who sends the prophets, as he declares, he must hold a position of authority over those whom he sends.

Where the prophets would have said, "Hear the word of the Lord," Jesus said, "Verily, verily, I say unto you" and proceeded to establish the word of the Lord. This expression could just as well have been translated, "Amen, Amen, I say unto you." We expect to find "Amen" at the end of a sermon. Jesus often used it to introduce what he was going to say. The difference is that the prophets were speaking in the name of God; he was speaking as God.[1]

As offensive as this practice was to the Jews, had Christ done anything less than speak by the authority of the Father, it could hardly have been supposed that he was the Hope of Israel, their long-sought Redeemer, the Savior of all mankind. The prophetic description of the Messiah recorded by Moses embraced the promise that he would speak the words God placed in his mouth (see Deuteronomy 18:18). In fulfillment of that promise, as Jesus concluded his earthly ministry, he reported to the Father, "I have given unto them the words which thou gavest me" (John 17:8).

It is true that Christ taught from the Jewish scriptures but only to the extent that those records had not been perverted (see JST Luke 11:53). He interpreted scripture by the Spirit of revelation, finding in them truths hidden from the understanding of their Jewish caretakers. He also meticulously observed the law of Moses but only as that law was given by Moses. He had no use for the uninspired trappings in which the Pharisees and rabbis had wrapped it (see Mark 7). He called them hypocrites and said they fit the words of Isaiah when he said: "This people draweth nigh unto me with their mouth, and honoureth me with their lips; but their heart is far from me. But in vain they do worship me, teaching for doctrines the commandments of men" (Matthew 15:8–9). He rejected the authority of the temple priests and yet submitted himself to the baptism of John, who had been ordained by an angel of the Lord to "overthrow the kingdom of the Jews" (D&C 84:28). Indeed, he described the religious leaders of his day as "whited sepulchres" (Matthew 23:27) and prefigured their destruction with the cursing of the fig tree (Mark 11:12–14, 20–24).

Christ stood independent of the wisdom of men, as have his people in all ages. The true followers of Christ do not seek justification for their faith in the doctrines or practices of others. While respecting the law and freely rendering unto Caesar that which was Caesar's (see Matthew 22:21), the Savior sought no alliance with earthly kingdoms. "God hath chosen the foolish things of the world to confound the wise; and God hath chosen the weak things of the world to confound the things which are mighty; and base things of the world, and things which are despised, hath God chosen, yea, and things which are not, to bring to naught things that are" (1 Corinthians 1:27–28). Such is the profile of Christ, "the messenger of salvation" (D&C 93:8), and such is the profile of all who truly come in his name.

THE MESSAGE OF SALVATION

Having given a brief profile of the Messenger of Salvation, let us now, in like manner, briefly profile the message of salvation. "Behold, mine house is a house of order, saith the Lord God, and not a house of confusion" (D&C 132:8). Could it be otherwise? Are the doctrines of salvation, like the creeds of men, to be the children of contention? Are they to be determined by the councils of men? Are they to rest upon philosophical speculations? Can they be in constant flux, ever changing? Are they for sale? Are they negotiable? Can they be contradictory? Are they to favor a chosen few? Do they justify persecution of the nonbeliever? Each affirmative answer given to such questions, as they have been given by historical Christianity, affirms anew our testimony of a universal apostasy.

"Will I accept of an offering, saith the Lord, that is not made in my name?" (D&C 132:9). Many have professed the right to speak for God and to perform ordinances in his name. Many of these profess the Bible as their source of authority. If the powers of heaven can be obtained in such a manner, what of civil authority? Would reverence for Blackstone's book of laws grant one the right to enter into treaties with other nations or empower one with the authority to bestow citizenship or, better still, to impose taxes? Would not a principle that made havoc of earthly governments have the same effect upon a heavenly one? Others profess a certificate of authority granted by a school or community. We ask, What school can empower its graduates to remit sins, resurrect the dead, and speak for God? In it all, we are left to wonder why people recognize the necessity of authority at all levels of society and in all kingdoms save only the kingdom of God, which announces itself to be a house of order.

"Will I receive at your hands that which I have not appointed? And will I appoint unto you, saith the Lord, except it be by law, even as I and my Father ordained unto you, before the world was?" (D&C 132:10–11). And so we have it: all principles of salvation must trace themselves directly to the God of heaven. Further, they must be absolute and eternal; that is, the price appended to heavenly treasures must be everlastingly the same. They cannot be granted to those of one age at a price either greater or lesser than that of another age.

Revelation both ancient and modern affirms that the gospel was taught to all the children of God long before their birth into mortality (see Alma 13:3; D&C 132:11). I have no recollection of such a thing, one may argue, but when the truths of salvation are declared, the honest in heart sense a distant echo from the past; the memory of the heart is quickened, and a reunion of spirits takes place. "My sheep hear my voice," the Savior declared. "I know them, and they follow me" (John 10:27). All people have been born with sufficient of the light of Christ to find their way to the waters of everlasting life and even to the fountainhead, if it is their desire to make the journey (see D&C 84:46–47).

THOSE WHO OPPOSED CHRIST

Among the Jews at the time of Christ, the source of divine authority was said to be the law of Moses and the oral traditions that were also traced to Sinai. "And the Lord said unto Moses, Write thou these words: for after the tenor of these words I have made a covenant with thee and with Israel" (Exodus 34:27). Thus the revelation of Sinai was held to be of two parts: the written law and the commentary on that which was written ("the tenor of these words"), which together were to constitute God's covenant with his chosen people. It was held that the oral law was faithfully transmitted from generation to generation in an unbroken chain: "Moses received the Law from Sinai and committed it to Joshua, and Joshua to the elders, and the elders to the Prophets; and the Prophets committed it to the men of the Great Synagogue."[2]

It was after the death of Christ and his apostles that the oral tradition was first committed to writing in the Mishnah and the Talmud. It was the oral tradition that made Pharisaism the source of authority in official Judaism. It was tradition, not the law, by which the rabbis made countless additions to the revelation of Sinai. The traditions were born, at least such was the pretense, as a fence around the law. They in turn gave birth to the scholarship of the rabbis, for only one well learned in the law could divine the multitude of traditions. Jacob, brother of Nephi, though a continent away, described by the Spirit of prophecy this pattern of apostasy: "The Jews were a stiffnecked people; and they despised the words of plainness, and killed the prophets, and sought for things that they could not understand. Wherefore, because of their blindness, which blindness came by looking beyond the mark, they must needs fall; for God hath taken away his plainness from them, and delivered unto them many things which they cannot understand, because they desired it. And because they desired it God hath done it, that they may stumble" (Jacob 4:14).

It was not the law given on Sinai that governed the people to whom Christ and his disciples preached but the traditions that like wild vines had overgrown it. "The Law—not the Law in its simplicity but the Law modified, transformed, distorted by Tradition—the Law robbed of its essential significance by the blind zeal which professed to defend it—became the centre of an abject servility. It came to be regarded as the only means of intercourse with God, and almost as the substitute for God. Immeasurable evils ensued. Piety dwindled into legalism. Salvation was identified with outward conformity."[3] Pharisaism reigned supreme. So important did study of religious traditions become that it would yet be said by one of the famed rabbis that God himself spent three hours a day studying Torah.[4]

The cycle of events is as easy to identify as the cycle of the seasons. That which had been written by the finger of God on Sinai was to govern the people, but someone must explain that which had been written. What does the Law mean and how is it to be applied? The oral tradition became the answer, giving definition and form to the law. Thus, what began as a supplement to the law was gradually substituted for it, and because the rabbis were the interpreters of tradition, they became the voice of God to his people. Farrar said it well: "Claiming too much for the Law the Rabbis left it too little. By adding to God's commandments so largely they also took from them. By imposing additional restrictions they broke down proper safeguards."[5]

When scribes succeeded prophets, tradition superseded priesthood, and revelation ceased. Liberty of thought was abrogated by the trained religious leader who stood between his people and the God of heaven. Instead of truth making people free, error made them slaves to an unyielding orthodoxy. The rabbinic yoke was much larger and heavier than the one forged by their Roman captors, for it dominated the whole existence of a person, intruding into even the most trivial actions of daily life. Thus Christ was rejected in the name of loyalty to the law that he himself had given as a preparatory gospel for him. Faced with the choice between loyalty to their traditions and hearkening to a Living Voice, the greater part of the people chose tradition.

It may be difficult to determine which is the most destructive to the soul, spiritual lethargy or excessive zeal, though it can be said that the chances are greater that the lethargic soul will awaken and correct his course than that the excessively zealous soul will seek an appropriate spiritual balance. Having declared the principles of salvation, the Savior warned: "And whoso shall declare more or less than this, and establish it for my doctrine, the same cometh of evil, and is not built upon my rock; but he buildeth upon a sandy foundation, and the gates of hell stand open to receive such when the floods come and the winds beat upon them" (3 Nephi 11:40).

THAT FOR WHICH WE LOOK

Having identified the three principles that combined to bring assurance to those of the meridian day, namely a credible source, a message of light and truth, and the opposition of the kingdom of darkness, we now proceed to the matter of applying those principles to our own day. We begin with the principle of a credible source. Following the scriptural pattern, we look for a prophet, one with the same rugged independence from the kingdoms and powers of the world that typified the prophets and apostles of both the Old and the New Testaments. We do not look for reformers. Theirs was a courageous work, but they did not profess the kind of authority that has been distinctive to those holding the prophetic office. Reformers speak for a disgruntled society; prophets speak for God. Similarly, we do not look for men of letters. The wisdom of men is hardly that of heaven. "My thoughts are not your thoughts, neither are your ways my ways, saith the Lord. For as the heavens are higher than the earth, so are my ways higher than your ways, and my thoughts than your thoughts" (Isaiah 55:8–9).

For whom, then, do we look? We look for someone who stands independent of extant religious traditions. We look for someone untutored in the ways of men but known to God. We look for someone who again can say, "Thus saith the Lord," someone whose knowledge of heavenly things comes not from books but from experience. We look for someone who dreams dreams, sees visions, entertains angels, pens scripture, and professes all spiritual gifts and signs that we have been assured will follow them that believe. And what of his message? How are we to know it? Given that truth is everlastingly the same, the message of a true messenger will accord with that spoken by all the holy prophets since the world began. Thus in one of the earliest revelations ever recorded we read these words: "I am God; I made the world, and men before they were in the flesh. . . . If thou wilt turn unto me, and hearken unto my voice, and believe, and repent of all thy transgressions, and be baptized, even in water, in the name of Mine Only Begotten Son, who is full of grace and truth, which is Jesus Christ, the only name which shall be given under heaven, whereby salvation shall come unto the children of men, ye shall receive the gift of the Holy Ghost, asking all things in his name, and whatsoever ye shall ask, it shall be given you" (Moses 6:51–52).

The economy of heaven is not in disarray, nor are the fruits of righteousness seasonal. With God there is constancy, and if God is the same, then the ordinances of salvation are the same, and the faith and obedience required for their purchase must be the same. And what then of the opposition to such truths? We have every assurance it too will be the same, for light and darkness will never meet.

LIGHT CLEAVETH UNTO LIGHT

There are so many forms of Christianity in the world today that it has been suggested that the term *Christianities* would be more accurate. It is generally supposed that this is a wholesome thing quite acceptable to the original Author. We will consider this matter in Chapter 8, but for the moment let it suffice to say that the Lord's house cannot be a house of confusion. There are no bargains where eternal principles are concerned. To suggest that such is the case is to change the principles. You can dress truth up in a variety of ways, but you cannot change it and still have it be the truth. Jesus of Nazareth marked a course for all humankind to follow. That path alone leads to the salvation he promised. To follow any other path, no matter how slight the change in direction may initially seem, is to pursue a different course and thus to follow a different Christ. There is no salvation in following false Christs.

What ought to be immediately identifiable as a corrupt form of Christianity is any doctrine that cannot bear examination—a doctrine shrouded in the guise of mystery or one that is so incomprehensible that even when pounded on an anvil cannot resemble anything that fell from the lips of the Savior or those commissioned by him. Light and truth are the glory of God, not darkness and ignorance. Certainly there are things we do not presently understand. Our life's labor is to reduce their number. What we don't do is worship them. When the wise men from the East sought the Christ Child, they followed the light of a heaven-sent star. Without that light they would have been left to wander in the dark.

THE TRUTHS OF SALVATION ARE ACCESSIBLE TO ALL

Two absolute and eternal truths are involved here. First, when matters of salvation are at stake, the channels through which the waters of everlasting life flow must be accessible to all. True it is that Moses ascended Sinai alone to stand in the presence of God, but having done so, he sought to sanctify his people that they might behold "the face of God" (D&C 84:20–24). The true test of a prophet is not in his conveying the revelations given him but in his qualifying his followers to receive their own. "Would God that all the Lord's people were prophets," Moses said, "and that the Lord would put his spirit upon them!" (Numbers 11:29). It was "a kingdom of priests, and an holy nation" that he sought to create (Exodus 19:6). Like Christ's, his doctrine was not "reverence me" but "follow me" (Matthew 4:19; 8:22; 9:9). There is nothing exclusive in the invitation to "ask of God," save it be done in sincerity and with real intent (see James 1:5–6; Moroni 10:4). The true and living God is no respecter of persons (see Acts 10:34).

Second, the truth of every revelation from heaven will be found within the revelation itself. Truth has its own spirit, and that spirit is identifiable to all who have eyes to see and ears to hear. The truths of salvation are not hidden in a heavenly monastery to be unveiled after our mortal sojourn. Eternal life is found in knowing God, not in ignorance of him (see John 17:3). The best defense of truth is simply to state it.

When a religious leader forbids members of his congregation to speak to those of other faiths, which frequently happens, we are left to wonder what he is hiding. Well might we ask, Has he left his parishioners without a message to share with others? Is their faith so frail that it does not bear examination? Only a false religion would demand acceptance without examination. True religion requires all to ask of God, for all must gain sufficient faith to stand and walk alone.

NOTES

1. See Xavier Léon-Dufour, trans. Terrence Prendegast, *Dictionary of the New Testament* (San Francisco: Harper & Row, 1983), p. 91; W. E. Vine, *An Expository Dictionary of New Testament Words* (New Jersey: Fleming H. Revell Co., 1966), p. 53; Geoffrey W. Bromiley, *Theological Dictionary of the New Testament* (Grand Rapids, Mich.: William B. Eerdmans Publishing, 1986), pp. 53–54.

2. Marcel Simon, trans. James H. Farley, *Jewish Sects at the Time of Jesus* (Philadelphia: Fortress Press, 1980), p. 35.

3. Frederic W. Farrar, *History of Interpretation* (Grand Rapids, Mich.: Baker Book House, 1979), p. 58.

4. Farrar, *History of Interpretation*, p. 60.

5. Farrar, *History of Interpretation*, p. 60.

Chapter Two

THE RULE OF FAITH

And this greater priesthood administereth the gospel and holdeth the key of the mysteries of the kingdom, even the key of the knowledge of God.
—*Doctrine and Covenants 84:19*

IN SCRIPTURE AND ALL TRUE theology, the word *faith* is used to link us with those principles that are assuredly and certainly true. The rule of faith is the message, the word, or the revelation upon which all else rests. The rule of faith is government by unalterable truths. Faith does not and cannot stand alone; it obtains life only as an expression of belief in a given principle. The power of faith comes from the principle to which it is appended. For instance, we do not properly speak of faith alone but rather of faith in Christ. Only when the object of faith becomes Christ does faith obtain the power of salvation. Were the object of our faith a falsehood, then the power accrued could only be that which comes from false or nonexistent principles.

If there are no absolute truths, no fixed principles that are the object of our faith, then there can be no faith. Our faith may be uncertain or weak, but the principle to which it is appended cannot. Thus faith cannot be exercised in principles that are untrue, nor can the principles in which it is exercised be changed. The spirit that directs self-styled intellectuals in their efforts to redefine established principles and thus change the rule of faith is the same spirit that motivated Lucifer in the grand Council in Heaven. Their efforts, like his, are to dispose of the plan of the Father for the salvation of his children in order to place themselves upon the throne of glory.

Let us consider what constitutes the rule of faith in Catholic, Protestant, and Latter-day Saint theology.

THE RULE OF FAITH AMONG CATHOLICS

Roman Catholic theology holds that Christian doctrine is revealed doctrine. The church acknowledges that human reason, the wonders of nature, and the hand of Providence all reveal the existence of God, but the revelation upon which the church claims to rest is a special and unique revelation received from Christ and the teachings of his apostles and prophets. Only in this revelation are those things necessary for salvation found. The idea that Rome teaches any doctrine that has not been received by revelation is emphatically repudiated. All revelation must trace itself to Christ or the Holy Ghost. Thus to treat any doctrine as uncertain is to be guilty of unbelief, and to treat any doctrine as secondary or as unimportant is to impugn the wisdom of the source from which it came.

The channels through which the revelation of Christ and his gospel came are said by Roman Catholics to be two: the scriptures and oral tradition. By scriptures is meant the Bible, including the fifteen intertestamental books generally known as the Apocrypha. By oral tradition is meant that body of teachings that are said to have been handed down orally from Christ and his apostles to succeeding generations. During the first century the only scripture available to the church was the Old Testament. That scripture and the testimony of the leaders governed the church. Many points of doctrine, worship, and discipline would have been left unanswered were it not for an oral tradition. Such a tradition was also necessitated by the obscurity of much that is in the scriptures. This tradition is believed to be wider in scope than the books of the New Testament, which the church subsequently collected and elevated to the status of scripture. The concept of oral tradition called upon a time when people remembered and related things concerning the Savior and his apostles that the writers of the New Testament did not record. In the first century, the spoken testimony of those professing a commission to preach the gospel of Christ rather than written records were of prime importance in the propagation of the gospel both in the congregation of believers and among investigators.[1]

Significantly, the Catholic claim to spiritual authority repeats the arguments used by the Jews from before the time of Christ, that is, scripture and tradition. In like manner, they too have come to acknowledge tradition as preeminent to scripture. That accounts for today's church bearing little resemblance to that of the New Testament. That in turn is seen simply as the result of the oral tradition being more fully developed than the written tradition. "The worship of the Apostolic age was without altars, without temples, without images; but as sacerdotal ideas entered and prevailed, ancient simplicity disappeared. The common meal, in which the early Christians united to commemorate their Savior's love, became a sacrifice; the table at which they sat to partake of it became an altar; the community which Christ designed to be one body, was divided into clergy and laity. When the liberty of prophesying was lost, and the spiritual gifts promised to the congregation were exercised by a restricted order of ministers alone, those ministers became priests; whilst the simple effusions of Gospel love prompted by the Holy

Spirit, and therefore powerful to break in pieces the stony and bind up the broken heart, were replaced by learned and eloquent discourses, which were even at times received with plaudits, as in a theater. Lastly the room or simple meeting-house was exchanged for a stately temple, rich furnished with gold and silver vessels."[2]

Critics have not been slow to point out that the Catholic claim to such a rich body of apostolic tradition is without historical evidence. That is to say, nothing survived the first or second centuries to sustain Catholic doctrines and practices. The most significant doctrinal pronouncements for which apostolic tradition is claimed as the source of authority came very late and only then after considerable contention within the ranks of the Church. If the Church was in possession of the answers, why the lengthy and fractious disputes? The parade example is their creedal statement about the nature of God, out of which the all-important doctrine of the Holy Trinity grows. Not only is the language unscriptural but we are without any evidence that any reference to apostolic tradition was made at the historic council of Nicaea in A.D. 325. Nor is any reference made to such a tradition during the generations of contention that followed. Five times Athanasius, the great champion of this doctrine, was banished as the winds of doctrine twisted and changed. As to infant baptism, we have no reference to it before the third century, and the doctrine of Purgatory was unknown before the end of the twelfth century.[3] As to the doctrine of immaculate conception, it had to wait until the year 1854 to be announced.[4] The point here is that if the church was in possession of a body of apostolic tradition by which such doctrinal pronouncements were to be made, it must at the same time be guilty of a grave dereliction of duty in withholding such knowledge from the understanding of the faithful for so many generations. It is difficult to argue, for instance, that the doctrine of immaculate conception is a point of faith, on the one hand, and on the other that the church was in possession of that knowledge for eighteen hundred years without acknowledging it.

To embrace the Catholic claim to authority requires that its adherents accept, without question, two propositions: first, that the church was indeed established by Christ and his apostles in the meridian of time; and second, that the church, through the years, has been true to the principles of its founder. Historical and doctrinal inquiry, however, is officially closed by an appeal to the dogma of infallibility, or the inability of the church to err in teaching revealed truth.[5] This determination was made at the First Vatican Council (1870), which "declared that the Pope was infallible when he defined that a doctrine concerning faith or morals was part of the deposit of divine revelation handed down from apostolic tradition and was therefore to be believed by the whole Church."[6]

The doctrine of infallibility is another doctrinal pronouncement that would have to trace itself to oral tradition, for neither the idea of a pope nor the idea of infallibility can be found in holy writ. If we are to bring into discussion the matter of the holiness and the divine character of the church, we would feel pressed to inquire why the heavenly power that is said to preside over such an institution would have such concern to maintain all tenets of belief as infallible while maintaining no such interest in the behavior of the church.[7]

THE RULE OF FAITH AMONG PROTESTANTS

The chief characteristic of Protestantism, one common to all its denominations, is the acceptance of the Bible as the only source of revealed truth. The conservative view of the Protestant norm of doctrine is expressed in the uncompromising formula that "the Bible, the whole Bible, and nothing but the Bible" is the religion of the Protestants. The view taken of the rule of faith among Protestant churches has also been to some extent a dividing factor. The alienation of the Reformed Church from the Lutheran was at least confirmed by a difference of attitude towards religious authority. The Lutherans were content to retain traditional elements so long as they did not conflict with scripture, whereas the churches of the Reformed group required scripture to justify anything that was accepted as part of the system of doctrine or worship.

In understanding the Protestant view, it is important to realize that the Reformers in proclaiming the scriptures to be the supreme standard[8] did not have in mind the whole Bible but rather the authority of the Bible as a whole when interpreted from its center—that is, a reinterpretation of everything in the Bible as seen through the lens of the Protestant doctrine of justification by faith alone. The Bible is a complex and in many ways contradictory book. No system of theology actively uses the whole of its contents; everyone chooses those parts of its revelation that they want to have stand center stage. The Reformers were no different. They chose certain passages from Paul through which they interpreted the place, value, and meaning of everything else. Thus the rest of the Bible assumes importance as it provides proof texts to that end or as it is seen to be instructive in sustaining traditional values. There is, of course, the haunting suspicion that both tradition and scripture have been believed for convenient reasons and that those reasons are the true fathers of the belief, not the traditions or the scriptures.

Four assumptions underlie the Protestant understanding of scripture, none of which is justified by scripture: authority, sufficiency, perspicuity (meaning clarity), and efficacy.[9] Let us briefly consider each.

First, authority. The scripture, meaning the Old and the New Testaments, constitutes the source of authority for the Protestant world. The authority of scripture is held to be exclusive, in contrast to the limited authority it is allowed in the Roman Catholic system. Maintaining this position rids the gospel message of the doctrines and practices that are not justified by scripture. Taking Martin Luther as a point of reference, it is important to note that he never sought to create a new church, least of all a Lutheran church. For Luther there was only one church, the Church of Christ. Luther held that the church had ceased to be catholic and had become papist instead. Basic doctrines, such as justification by faith, the true meaning of the Lord's supper, the priesthood of all believers, and the authority of scripture, he felt, had been neglected, and other doctrines had been added in their stead. These included penance, the mass, papal infallibility, indulgences, and the interdict (the barring of a person or place from ecclesiastical functions).[10] To find the original plan of worship, it was argued, one had to go back to the New Testament. "No man can get nearer the source than that. It was the ultimate, objective, historical authority, the criterion of all judgment, the canon or norm by which we are to live." This meant that all humanly devised innovations were to be discarded. This back-to-the-scripture movement was to be a *re-formation* of that which had suffered a *de-formation*. Luther's desire was not for some kind of idyllic pattern of church life (which never existed in New Testament times) but to return to a true apostolic doctrine. What Luther sought was a church that the apostles would have known and recognized had they been allowed to return to the sixteenth century. Lutherans were to be the successors of the apostolic church.[11]

All the reformers of the sixteenth century, German, Swiss, and British alike, believed that God had spoken to them through the scriptures. They believed that every man, woman, and child, if granted access to the scriptures, could enjoy that same revelation and thus through the scripture have immediate access to God. *Sola scriptura*, the scriptures only, is the doctrine that binds all the branches of the Reformation together. What cannot be proved from scripture has no authority in the church. When Martin Luther faced the emperor at Worms in 1521, he concluded the defense of his faith:

"Unless I am convinced by the testimony of Scripture, or evident reason (for I put my faith neither in Pope nor Councils as authorities in themselves, since it is established that they have often erred and contradicted one another), I am bound by the scriptural authorities cited by me, and my conscience is captive to the Word of God; I will recant nothing and cannot do so, since it is neither safe nor honest to do ought against conscience. Here I stand! I can do no other! God help me. Amen."[12]

Two primary concerns are raised by the doctrine of *sola scriptura*. First, the moment Luther claimed that the authority of the Bible superseded that of the tradition of the Church, he invited criticism because the selection of books that constitute the Bible were determined by nothing other than tradition! No revelation identifies them or even directs that they be gathered together. The church was the father of the Bible, not the child. That is to say, if there had been no church with its traditions, there would have been no Bible as Martin Luther knew it. The question then challenging Luther was how he could accept one line of tradition as inspired while rejecting the other. Second, the doctrine of *sola scriptura* makes Bible worshipers of its adherents. The Catholics claim an infallible pope; the Protestants counter with the claim to an infallible book. For them the scriptures, not God, are the Supreme Judge of all things.

Next, we turn our attention to the doctrine of sufficiency, or the doctrine that holds that the Bible contains and makes known all that is necessary to salvation. Again, two paramount concerns suggest themselves. First, this doctrine seals the heavens and imposes upon God a vow of silence that neither scripture nor God ever intended; and second, it assures that the true meaning of that scripture will be lost, for that which comes by revelation can only be properly understood by revelation. None has stated it better than Nephi, who warned: "Wo be unto him that shall say: We have received the word of God, and we need no more of the word of God, for we have enough! For behold, thus saith the Lord God: I will give unto the children of men line upon line, precept upon precept, here a little and there a little; and blessed are those who hearken unto my precepts, and lend an ear unto my counsel, for they shall learn wisdom; for unto him that receiveth I will give more; and from them that shall say, We have enough, from them shall be taken away even that which they have" (2 Nephi 28:29–30).

The third assumption is that of perspicuity, or clarity. The idea is that the scriptures are sufficiently clear, that neither the church nor tradition is necessary to properly interpret them. That is not to deny that some passages are difficult to understand but rather to avow that in the general tenor of its teaching as it pertains to our salvation the message of the Bible is clear and that difficult passages can be understood with the help of those which are plain. Thus the doctrine is that scripture is its own interpreter.

The official policy of the church during the thirteenth and fourteenth centuries was to condemn Bible societies and to regard unrestricted access to the scriptures as both a danger to laymen's souls and a challenge to the authority of the church. Luther, for instance, had never seen a Bible before he entered the monastery, and when he was there, he was discouraged from reading it. Nathin, his mentor, told him that it would only breed unrest and thus tried to divert him to a study of church traditions.[13] It was in opposition to such practices that Protestantism affirmed so vigorously the efficacy of scripture and promoted the circulation of the Bible in the common tongue.

In actual practice there is little to sustain the doctrine of biblical perspicuity. The doctrine of scriptural plainness and clarity is called upon to sustain the indescribable mystery of the Trinity, which can only be arrived at by rejecting the plain meaning of hosts of scriptural texts that must be declared metaphorical. No lay reader without the aid of a trained minister would ever have arrived at the notion that Christ was actually his own father. Nor would they suppose the plain statements relative to baptism could be supplanted by a profession of faith, or the countless texts sustaining the necessity of good works be superseded by the dogma of justification by grace alone. Who among the readers of the Bible in times past would have supposed that in a future day both those supporting and those opposing homosexual and lesbian movements could sustain their cause with scriptural arguments?

And finally, the doctrine of efficacy, which is the claim that the truth and goodness of the Bible are self-evident. Though true, such a claim is not without its own bounds or limits. In response to a skeptic, reformer John Calvin frankly admitted that he knew of no scriptural argument that would convince him so long as he chose to maintain a carnal nature and an unspiritual mind.[14] The believer can adduce arguments that are weighty enough to justify faith in scripture, but they have not the force of a mathematical proof for the mind of the natural man. Scripture is convincing only to the convinced. Paul said it well: "Eye hath not seen, nor ear heard, neither have entered into the heart of man, the things which God hath prepared for them that love him. But God hath revealed them unto us by his Spirit: for the Spirit searcheth all things, yea, the deep things of God. For what man knoweth the things of a man, save the spirit of man which is in him? even so the things of God knoweth no man, but the Spirit of God" (1 Corinthians 2:9–11).

No principle of truth can retain its meaning in isolation from other truths. Faith must be anchored to Christ, baptism must be preceded by repentance, mercy cannot rob justice, and so forth. So it is with the Bible. It finds its true meaning only in the Spirit of revelation. In the hands of a scoundrel, it becomes the source of endless mischief.

THE RULE OF FAITH AMONG LATTER-DAY SAINTS

Mormonism stands independent of the claims to authority professed by either Catholicism or Protestantism. Singularly, it does so while embracing the Bible as God's word. Yet it rejects the Catholic claim of an apostolic tradition and the Protestant claim of Bible sufficiency. Apostolic tradition is unnecessary in a church that has living apostles, as is the need to depend on revelations given to dispensations past. A written record of God's word was never sufficient for those who had the power to obtain revelations of their own. This was the case with those of whom we read in the Bible. We dare not rest the hope of our salvation on the tangled vines of tradition, nor do we suppose that a living church can be led by a written record.

"We believe all that God has revealed, all that He does now reveal, and we believe that He will yet reveal many great and important things pertaining to the Kingdom of God" (Articles of Faith 9). We place no limitations or bounds on what God can reveal to us. Some have supposed that God can do or say nothing that cannot be sustained or justified by some Bible texts. The Latter-day Saints do not worship a God who is bound in such a manner. Indeed, we anticipate a future day when things not yet seen nor heard by mortals, things that have not yet entered into the heart of mankind shall be revealed (see D&C 76:5–10). "God shall give unto you knowledge by his Holy Spirit," we have been promised, "yea, by the unspeakable gift of the Holy Ghost, that has not been revealed since the world was until now;

"Which our forefathers have awaited with anxious expectation to be revealed in the last times, which their minds were pointed to by the angels, as held in reserve for the fulness of their glory;

"A time to come in the which nothing shall be withheld, whether there be one God or many gods, they shall be manifest.

"All thrones and dominions, principalities and powers, shall be revealed and set forth upon all who have endured valiantly for the gospel of Jesus Christ.

"And also, if there be bounds set to the heavens or to the seas, or to the dry land, or to the sun, moon, or stars—

"All the times of their revolutions, all the appointed days, months, and years, and all the days of their days, months, and years, and all their glories, laws, and set times, shall be revealed in the days of the dispensation of the fulness of times—

"According to that which was ordained in the midst of the Council of the Eternal God of all other gods before this world was, that should be reserved unto the finishing and the end thereof, when every man shall enter into his eternal presence and into his immortal rest" (D&C 121:26–32).

The revelations now known to the Latter-day Saints are but a pittance compared to what we expect to receive. Joseph Smith taught the principle thus: "How long can rolling waters remain impure? What power shall stay the heavens? As well might man stretch forth his puny arm to stop the Missouri river in its decreed course, or to turn it up stream, as to hinder the Almighty from pouring down knowledge from heaven upon the heads of the Latter-day Saints" (D&C 121:33).

WHERE WE MUST STAND

We claim no priesthood, keys, power, authority, or doctrines that do not trace themselves directly to heaven. We have not built upon the theological rubble of the past. All that we have, and this includes our faith in the Bible and our understanding of it, has come to us by direct revelation in this dispensation. Doctrines from any other source are without authority among the Latter-day Saints. All doctrine and authority must come through the channels the Lord has ordained for our dispensation, and that channel is the priesthood and keys restored to the Prophet Joseph Smith. "The Melchizedek Priesthood," he said, "is the channel through which all knowledge, doctrine, the plan of salvation and every important matter is revealed from heaven."[15] The Melchizedek Priesthood administers the gospel and holds the key of the mysteries of heaven and the key of the knowledge of God (see D&C 84:19).

The essence of virtually every argument directed against Mormonism centers on the critics' refusal to acknowledge that revelation, as known to the ancients, can be had in our day. Paradoxically, most of these critics profess a preference for the revelations of dispensations past. They claim those revelations as their own, declaring that the Spirit speaks to them through the ancient writings. What they cannot tolerate is the thought that God could speak anew, that other words could be penned that are of equal worth to those of an ancient day, and that those words should rightly be added to the canon of scripture. They profess prophets, but not living prophets; they reverence revelation, but only that revelation given to another people in another time.

I have an indelible memory of a family night held a few days before I was to leave to serve in the military in Vietnam. I listened that evening as my father gave inspired blessing to my brothers. Each was given wise counsel and remarkable promises. I could not help coveting the promises they were receiving, and I prayed in my heart that I too could be so blessed. But because I had received a special blessing from my father when he set me apart to be a missionary, I did not think he would give me another blessing. Thankfully, he chose to do so. That blessing, like those given to my brothers, was distinctively personal. The nature of the counsel and promises were different, for they were mine and were thus suited to my circumstances.

So it is with the revelations of this dispensation. We may desire to steal some of the promises given to the ancients, but the greater blessing is always that which is distinctively our own. It is the one suited to our circumstances and needs. Thus as Latter-day Saints we have neither borrowed our doctrines nor our understanding of them from the ancients. Our doctrines and authority all bear the label of modern revelation. Our God speaks directly to people of this day. Such is the message that we seek to declare to all the world. The living voice of God constitutes our rule of faith.

NOTES

1. See W. P. Paterson, *The Rule of Faith* (London: Hodder and Stoughton, 1912), pp. 31–35.

2. Edward Backhouse, *Early Church History to the Death of Constantine,* ed. Charles Tylor (London, 1884), pp. 417–18.

3. See Jacques Le Goff, *The Birth of Purgatory,* trans. Arthur Goldhammer (Chicago: University of Chicago Press, 1984), p. 4.

4. See F. L. Cross, ed., *The Oxford Dictionary of the Christian Church* (Oxford: Oxford University Press, 1990), p. 692.

5. Paterson, *Rule of Faith,* pp. 35–37.

6. Cross, *Oxford Dictionary of the Christian Church,* p. 701.

7. Paterson, *Rule of Faith,* p. 43.

8. The Westminster Confession of Faith states the matter thus: "The whole counsel of God, concerning all things necessary for his own glory, man's salvation, faith, and life, is either expressly set down in scripture, or by good and necessary consequence may be deduced from scripture: unto which nothing at any time is to be added, whether by new revelations of the Spirit, or traditions of men" (chap. 1, sec. 6). "The supreme Judge, by which all controversies of religion are to be determined, and all decrees of councils, opinions of ancient writers, doctrines of men, and private spirits, are to be examined, and in whose sentence we are to rest, can be no other but the Holy Spirit speaking in the scriptures" (chap. 1, sec. 10). *Westminster Confession of Faith* (Inverness, Scotland: John G. Eccles Printers, Ltd., 1983), pp. 22, 24.

9. Paterson, *Rule of Faith,* p. 59.

10. An interdict is an ecclesiastical punishment in the Roman Catholic Church that excludes a member or a community of members from participating in spiritual things without loss of membership. For instance, Pope Alexander III placed Scotland under interdict for the expulsion of the bishop of St. Andrews.

11. See James Atkinson, *Martin Luther, Prophet to the Church Catholic* (Grand Rapids, Mich.: William B. Eerdmans Publishing, Paternoster Press, 1983), pp. 141–42.

12. Atkinson, *Martin Luther,* p. 149.

13. Atkinson, *Martin Luther,* pp. 157–58.

14. Paterson, *Rule of Faith,* p. 67.

15. Joseph Smith, *Teachings of the Prophet Joseph Smith,* sel. Joseph Fielding Smith (Salt Lake City: Deseret Book, 1974), pp. 166–67.

Chapter Three

THE BIBLE SAYS

In the midst of this war of words and tumult of opinions, I often said to myself: what is to be done? Who of all these parties are right; or, are they all wrong together? If any one of them be right, which is it, and how shall I know it? . . .

The teachers of religion of the different sects understood the same passages of scripture so differently as to destroy all confidence in settling the question by an appeal to the Bible.
—Joseph Smith–History 1:10, 12

THE OFTEN-HEARD PHRASE "the Bible says" may well have been used to introduce more nonsense and falsehood than any other three words ever uttered. There are more devils quoting scripture than prophets because there are more devils than prophets. If divine sanction can be obtained simply by quoting scripture, we need no longer distinguish between good and evil, for it is all the same. An instrument made by a master craftsman does not of itself bring forth great music. So it is with the words of the Bible. To call forth its message, one must stand in the light.

Just what value do we place on those declarations that have been prefaced by the words "the Bible says"? Are we to suppose that in the hands of a scoundrel the Bible is going to be used to further the cause of truth? May not its words be quoted by false Christs and false prophets? A book may *speak* of integrity, but a book does not *have* integrity. In like manner, a book may recount acts of faith, but a book does not have faith. A man is not virtuous simply because he possesses a book on virtue. Books, the Bible included, are simply black ink on white paper. It is for us to breathe into them the breath of life.

Let us consider some of the myths commonly associated with the Bible.

Myth I

THE BIBLE IS A SINGLE BOOK

When we hear someone say, "The Bible says . . . ," perhaps our response ought to be, "What Bible? The Jewish Bible, the Catholic Bible, the Protestant Bible?" Each differs markedly from the others. This myth centers on the notion that the Bible is a single book, when in fact it is a collection of books. The word *Bible* comes from the Greek *ta biblia,* which means "the books." Thus the "Holy Bible" is a collection of religious writings that have been gathered together over thousands of years. The process of collecting these books did not involve a universal agreement about which books ought to be included and which excluded from the sacred collection. The very fact that Jews, Catholics, and Protestants do not use the same books is evidence of it.

The library of holy writings was originally a collection of scrolls. More than two hundred years after the last scroll of the Christian Bible had been written, the Romans developed a *codex,* or a compilation of leaf pages. Only thereafter could the content of a collection of scrolls be bound together. A passage often used to sustain the argument that the canon of scripture was intended to be closed is the statement in the last chapter of the book of Revelation that warns against adding anything to that book (see Revelation 22:18). Though translators have chosen to use the word *book* in this and like texts, a more accurate rendering would be *scroll*. John's reference was to the scroll on which he was writing, not the collection of books we know as the Bible.

Today's Jewish Bible has twenty-four books known to Christians as the Old Testament. The Christian world has adopted these books but divides them so they number thirty-nine and has ordered them differently.[1] Interestingly, there was no general agreement among Jews about which books were considered canonical until after the events recorded in the New Testament had taken place. That decision was made at a council held at Jamnia (near Joppa in Israel) about A.D. 90. It was, we are told, "a tumultuous assemblage, and in the faction fights of the Rabbinic parties, blood was shed by their scholars. Hence the decision was regarded as irrevocable and sealed by blood."[2] The Septuagint, or Greek translation of the Old Testament, which had been surrounded with myths designed to sustain its claim to divine origin, was thereafter rejected by the Jews. Its use is now regarded as a more sorrowful event in Jewish history than the worship of the golden calf. The Septuagint was the child of the Diaspora and strongly reflected the influence of Greek thought. It embraced the fifteen intertestamental books known to us today as the Apocrypha. Those books were not a part of the Hebrew tradition and no longer find a place in the Jewish Bible, though they have found their way into the Catholic Bible.

The Catholic world has favored the books of the Apocrypha because they contain at least vague references that can be used to sustain the otherwise unscriptural doctrines of masses for the dead and purgatory (2 Maccabees 12:43–45). The Protestant world rejects them as scripture because they do not sustain the Protestant dogma of salvation by grace. When Joseph Smith asked the Lord if he should include them in his inspired translation, he was told that they contained much that was true and much that was not, and it was not necessary for him to translate them. The Lord also told Joseph Smith that though there were some translation difficulties with the Apocrypha, the greater problem was "interpolation by the hands of men," meaning that designing people had tampered with the texts (see D&C 91).

It ought be asked, What about the twenty-seven books that constitute our New Testament? By what authority were they chosen? And who assumed the prerogative to declare that they constitute the cessation of revelation? The story is both interesting and strangely paradoxical.

Two second-century heretics get leading roles in the drama: one for being the first to close the canon of scripture, and the second for causing the church to declare the heavens closed by maintaining that he was the Holy Ghost. Macrion, a bishop's son and a wealthy shipowner, was the first to create a list of canonical books. His Bible was closed to all but ten of the epistles of Paul and the Gospel of Luke, from which he had taken all references to the Jews. He rejected the Old Testament in its entirety because of its Jewish origins. Jesus, according to Macrion, was not born but sprang, like Zeus, fully grown from God. He came to earth to preach a ministry of redemption as a God of love in contrast with the capricious and cruel God of the Old Testament. So final was Macrion's excommunication from the church that even the money he had donated was returned.[3] This threat to the church was followed by another known to its followers as "the New Prophecy" and to history as "Montanism," after its founder, Montanus, a convert to Christianity from the province of Phrygia in Asia Minor. On the eve of his crucifixion, the Savior had told his disciples that he had many things to teach them but they could not bear them at that time. He then promised that the Holy Ghost would guide them "into all truth" and show them "things to come" (John 16:12–14). Montanus denounced the lack of revelation and the absence of spiritual gifts in the church. In doing so he claimed himself to be the advocate promised by the Savior and said that he had come to give them the promised revelation.[4]

Through the course of years, the church solved the problem of dealing with such heretics by announcing that revelation had ceased and that the canon of scripture was closed. Thus the biblical promise of continued revelation led the church of the second century to deny continuing revelation, while the idea of the Bible as a single, sacred, unalterable corpus of texts, which began as a heresy, was adopted in the efforts of the church to define orthodoxy.[5]

The Roman and other western churches used a New Testament of twenty-two books for at least a hundred years. Origen, an Alexandrian scholar, divided the books in his own New Testament into two classes: the acknowledged books and the disputed ones. His list of disputed books included James, 2 and 3 John, 2 Peter, Jude, the Letter of Barnabas, and the Shepherd of Hermas. These, with the other books known to the Bible reader, constituted the oldest Greek manuscript. It consisted of twenty-nine books.

Seventy-five years after the death of Origen, another eastern Christian, Eusebius of Caesarea, omitted the Shepherd and Barnabas from the canonical list. The great issue of that era was the reliability of the book of Revelation. Most Greek manuscripts of the New Testament omit it. Other disputed books from the New Testament, which Eusebius himself rejected, were the Acts of Paul, the Revelation of Peter, and the Teachings of the Apostles, all of which have remained in exile.

Another voice from that ancient day was that of Athanasius, the great champion of the dogma of the Trinity. It was his custom to write an Easter letter to the churches of his diocese. His letter written in A.D. 367 listed the books approved for reading in the church. His list, which is the same as our New Testament, is the earliest reference we have to a general acceptance of that particular grouping of texts.

Myth II

THE BIBLE PRECEDED DOCTRINE

It is generally held among those who claim membership in the traditional Christian churches that their doctrines originated with the Bible. As we have already seen, that could not have been the case, simply because the Bible did not exist until long after the creation of the church. If we hold that the church was organized by Christ or his apostles, then its organization came before any New Testament books were written. The book was created by the church, not the church by the book.

After the deaths of the apostles, there was no central leadership in the church. The Gospels, the epistles of Paul, and other writings that constitute the New Testament would for various reasons have been inaccessible to many branches of the church. Further, those in circulation would have shared the attention of various congregations with a variety of other manuscripts posing as scripture which have, as judged by history, fallen far short of the mark. These various branches, all calling themselves Christian, simply went their own way.

When Constantine decided to use the Christian church to unite the Roman Empire, he found it necessary first to unite Christendom. To that end he convened the first council of the church, by the authority of the state, at his palace in Nicaea in A.D. 325. The Council of Nicaea, to which all traditional Christian creeds trace themselves, convened to determine whether the Father and the Son could properly be thought of as being separate and distinct or whether orthodoxy demanded that it be believed they were of the same essence. The council determined that they were of the same essence, or that Jesus was his own father. Significantly, this monumental doctrinal announcement came after it had been declared that revelation had ceased but before there was agreement on what books constituted the closed canon.

Myth III

TRUE RELIGION IS BIBLE RELIGION

There are those who boast that their religion is Bible religion. Ironically, such a belief is unbiblical. Those so declaring ought to be reminded that no one who lived within the time period of the Bible ever had a Bible. Therefore, their religion was not Bible religion. If we follow their example, our religion cannot be Bible religion, either.

The Bible is not religion; it is a history of those who had religion. The religion of those who live within the covers of the Bible centered in living oracles and the ordinances of salvation. Theirs was a religion of prophets and apostles. It was a religion of continuous revelation, one in which they enjoyed the companionship of the Holy Ghost, entertained angels, dreamed dreams, and performed miracles. It was not a religion that centered on the declarations of prophets made at earlier times to another people. Such records were reverenced as scripture but were always subordinate to the voice of the living prophet. The faith of those of whom we read in the Bible centered on experiences that were immediate and personal.

Those within the Bible to which we turn for divine guidance never claimed direction from the revelations given to previous generations. They always stood as independent witnesses of the principles they taught. They knew God in ways other than by hearsay.

In Bible times such was expected. Today, for all of our knowledge, we could not, in a court of law or any place requiring rigorous proof, trace any book on the shelves of our libraries to the hand of its original writer in ancient Athens, Rome, or Jerusalem. We have no signed documents, no signatures of witnesses, no original manuscripts. Neither the Bible nor the Koran can comply with the rules of evidence that would allow its testimony to be admitted in a court of law. Without revelation in our day the revelation of the past is simply hearsay.

When the salvation of men is at stake, a more sure path is required than the one claimed by those whose religion centers on the Bible alone. Nor is it insignificant how perfectly the Book of Mormon marks such a path. Consider the testimony of Alma as he describes the authority by which he preached: "I am called," he said, "according to the holy order of God, which is in Christ Jesus; yea, I am commanded to stand and testify unto this people the things which have been spoken by our fathers [clearly referring to the scriptures]." Then he adds, and this is profoundly important, "This is not all. Do ye not suppose that I know of these things myself? Behold, I testify unto you that I do know that these things whereof I have spoken are true. And how do ye suppose that I know of their surety? Behold, I say unto you they are made known unto me by the Holy Spirit of God." He then explains that he had fasted and prayed many days to obtain that personal understanding. Thus he is able to say, "It has thus been revealed unto me, that the words which have been spoken by our fathers are true." Then, to assure us of the verity of what he has said, he begins to prophesy by that same Spirit. This, he said, is what constitutes the "holy order of God" (Alma 5:43–49).

Alma's description of how one comes to a knowledge of the plan of salvation is perfect. We start, as he did, with extant revelation— whether it be written or oral matters not. We seek through fasting and prayer to obtain the Spirit's witness of the verity of what we have been given, knowing that when we obtain that Spirit, it will lead us into an understanding of what we have been given and then, as appropriate, lead us beyond it. Rather than claiming the Bible as their religion, the ancients, of whom we read in the Bible, claimed continuous communication with the heavens as the source of their religion. Thus it becomes an everlasting principle that light will cleave to light, and that those having the truths of salvation will have light and truth added to them until that perfect day, in which they will enjoy the fulness of the Father (see D&C 50:24; 93:19–20).

Myth IV

EVERYTHING IN THE BIBLE IS THE WORD OF GOD

That the Bible contains the word of God is beyond question. That every word in the Bible was spoken by God is a sorrowful myth. Brigham Young identified this myth when he said: "I have heard ministers of the gospel declare that they believed every word in the Bible was the word of God. I have said to them 'you believe more than I do. I believe the words of God are there; I believe the words of the devil are there; I believe that the words of men and the words of angels are there; and that is not all,—I believe that the words of a dumb brute are there. I recollect one of the prophets riding, and prophesying against Israel, and the animal he rode rebuked his madness."[5]

In my experience, those who are the most adamant in declaring the Bible to be the word of God are also those who most freely press the Bible to mean and say things it clearly does not. An anti-Mormon book that uses the title *God's Word Final, Infallible, and Forever* gives its readers three standards that, if followed, will assure that they will not be caught in the Mormon net. Each of these standards, we are to assume, is rooted in the Bible. First, as readers we are warned not to pray about the message; after all, it is reasoned, people have been deceived by their prayers. The second warning is not to trust our feelings, because, we are told, feelings can also be deceptive. The third warning is not to trust our minds, for "our minds are reprobate."[6] So, the book concludes, if we refuse to pray, to trust our feelings, and to use our minds, there is no chance the Mormons will get us. (That was the only conclusion in a lengthy book with which I was able to agree.) What then are we to trust?

The answer is, of course, the Bible. What is really meant by this answer is the interpretation of selected passages of the Bible as given by the fellow who is claiming it to be "the word of God." At issue here is whether the Bible is still the word of God in the countless instances in which it directs us to pray and encourages us to use our hearts and minds. Did not the Savior himself command us, saying, "Ask, and it shall be given you; seek, and ye shall find; knock, and it shall be opened unto you: for everyone that asketh receiveth; and he that seeketh findeth; and to him that knocketh it shall be opened"? (Matthew 7:7–8). Is this not an invitation to pray for knowledge and understanding? And did he not condemn those of his day for rejecting their feelings and failing to use their minds when he said: "This people's heart is waxed gross, and their ears are dull of hearing, and their eyes they have closed [is this not the refusal to use both their hearts and their minds?]; lest at any time they should see with their eyes, and hear with their ears, and should understand with their heart, and should be converted, and I should heal them"? (Matthew 13:15). Significantly, modern renderings of this verse insert the word *minds* into the text. For instance, Today's English Version reads:

> you will look and look, but not see,
> because this people's minds are dull,
> and they have stopped up their ears,

and have closed their eyes.
Otherwise, their eyes would see,
   their ears would hear,
   their minds would understand,
and they would turn to me, says God,
   and I would heal them.[7]

Caution should be used in making claims for the Bible which it does not make for itself. Not once in the Bible does it refer to itself as the word of God. Certain utterances are referred to as his word, and we regard them as such. They are, however, very specific instances and, in almost every case, are spoken, or oral. For that matter the word *bible* is not used in the Bible, and nowhere within the covers of the book is any suggestion made as to what writings should be considered scripture and what things should not be so considered. What constitutes scripture is left undefined, and no book in the Bible refers to itself as such. The characters and writers of the New Testament frequently quote from Old Testament books in such a manner as to indicate they esteem them as scripture. They also give that same status to some books that have not survived as part of the canon (see Jude 1:9, 14–15).[8]

Without question the hand of the Lord has been over the Bible to protect and preserve it. Had that not been the case, its sacred message would have been completely lost to us. This is not to say, however, that it is unblemished or unscarred. Even if we were to concede that every word in it was of divine origin, those words would cease to be such in the hands of any whose purity and inspiration was less than that of those who originally penned the words. The word of God as interpreted by uninspired men ceases to be the word of God (see D&C 50:17–23). It does not make them spokesmen for the Lord, nor will its promises admit them into his divine presence.

Myth V

THE CANON IS CLOSED

"The whole counsel of God, concerning all things necessary for his own glory, man's salvation, faith, and life, is either expressly set down in scripture, or by good and necessary consequence may be deduced from scripture: unto which nothing at any time is to be added, whether by new revelations of the Spirit, or traditions of men." So declares the Westminster Confession.[9] That doctrine of sufficiency extends the "my religion is Bible religion" myth to embrace the idea that everything necessary for the salvation of men is found in the Bible as it presently stands, and nothing need be or can be added to it. One great difficulty with this myth is that there is no general agreement among those who use it about what the Bible means. Another significant difficulty is that the Bible itself does not sustain the myth. Nowhere in that compilation of sacred books does it say that no other books can be added to the compilation. Responding to this issue, Joseph Smith asked, "Does it remain for a people who never had faith enough to call down one scrap of revelation from heaven, and for all they have now are indebted to the faith of another people who lived hundreds and thousands of years before them, does it remain for them to say how much God has spoken and how much He has not spoken? We have what we have, and the Bible contains what it does contain: but to say that God never said anything more to man than is there recorded, would be saying at once that we have at last received a revelation: for it must require one to advance thus far, because it is nowhere said in that volume by the mouth of God, that He would not, after giving what is there contained, speak again; and if any man has found out for a fact that the Bible contains all that God ever revealed to man he has ascertained it by an immediate revelation, other than has been previously written by the prophets and apostles."[10]

Many claims are made for the Bible that it does not make for itself. Nowhere does it suggest that those who read it thereby obtain the commission to go forth and represent the Master, preaching his gospel or performing the ordinances of salvation. Nowhere does it declare an end to the principle of revelation or advocate the dogma of a closed canon. Nowhere does it declare itself to be the repository of the "whole counsel of God," nor does it declare itself to be inerrant or infallible. We are left to ask, "Is it not unbiblical to impose doctrines or dogmas on the Bible that it does not teach?"

Is it not somewhat ironic that God himself can no longer speak in what is supposed to be his own church? Is it not strange that a theology claiming the word of angels and prophets as its very foundation refuses now to admit the existence of either? To declare the Bible supreme in all matters of faith is dangerously close to (if distinguishable from) worship of the Bible. The following exchange between a friend and a scholar of another faith illustrates the danger here. My friend was challenged with the statement that there is no way in all the world that Latter-day Saints could ever justify the practice of polygamy. "Look," my friend responded, "if the God of heaven personally appeared to you and directed you to practice polygamy, wouldn't you do it?" "No," was the response, "even if God himself commanded it, I would not do it, because it is not found in the Bible!"

The Westminster Confession of Faith states the matter well: "The supreme Judge, by which all controversies of religion are to be determined, and all decrees of councils, opinions of ancient writers, doctrines of men, and private spirits, are to be examined, and in whose sentence we are to rest, can be no other but the Holy Spirit speaking in the scripture."[11] The Bible, not God, is being named the "supreme Judge" in such a declaration. In so saying I am aware that the immediate response will be that I have misread and that the intent is that "the Holy Spirit" is the "supreme Judge" as it speaks to us through the Bible. But this is not what is being said and it is not what is being practiced in adhering to such a philosophy.

I heard a rabbi explain this theory once. He told us that the ancient scriptures speak to us "with a fresh spirit" so that they are always applicable in telling us what God would have us know. Yet for him, those same scriptures preclude his turning a light switch on or off on the Sabbath day and have failed to prepare him to accept Jesus of Nazareth as the Messiah promised his people. Such excessive devotion to the light of an ancient time leaves many of our day in the dark. And how is it that the scriptures speak to us "with a fresh spirit"? John Henry Cardinal Newman in his classic *An Essay on the Development of Christian Doctrine* observes that scripture cannot be confined to its "mere literal interpretation." Were it not for the practice of giving a mystical interpretation of scripture, there would be no defense for such doctrines as celibacy, purgatory, or the doctrine of the Holy Trinity, he explains. "It may be almost laid down as an historical fact, that the mystical interpretation and orthodoxy will stand or fall together."[12] What we are being told here is that what the scriptures say has little to do with the orthodoxy of modern Christendom. Rather, orthodoxy is the result of a "mystical interpretation" of scriptures, which gives them a meaning far different from that suggested by the language in which they are written.

The idea that the Holy Spirit can speak through extant scripture is beyond question. The idea that the Holy Spirit is to be confined to that medium for its expression is itself unscriptural. The greater danger here is addressed by Nephi: "Yea, wo be unto him that saith: We have received, and we need no more!

"And in fine, wo unto all those who tremble, and are angry because of the truth of God! For behold, he that is built upon the rock receiveth it with gladness; and he that is built upon a sandy foundation trembleth lest he shall fall.

"Wo be unto him that shall say: We have received the word of God, and we need no more of the word of God, for we have enough!

"For behold, thus saith the Lord God: I will give unto the children of men line upon line, precept upon precept, here a little and there a little; and blessed are those who hearken unto my precepts, and lend an ear unto my counsel, for they shall learn wisdom; for unto him that receiveth I will give more; and from them that shall say, We have enough, from them shall be taken away even that which they have" (2 Nephi 28:27–30).

The principle is plain. To declare the heavens sealed and the canon closed is to lose at the same time the very power by which the scriptures must be understood. No scriptural text can be properly taught or learned save it be by that same Spirit by which it was revealed in the first place. "That which is of God is light; and he that receiveth light, and continueth in God, receiveth more light; and that light groweth brighter and brighter until the perfect day" (D&C 50:24).

Myth VI

THE BIBLE CAN BE INTERPRETED
INDEPENDENT OF A PREDETERMINED IDEOLOGY

Suppose that an angel of the Lord took the Bible (in this instance, meaning the traditional Christian Bible) to a people who had no previous knowledge of it and directed them to read it and then form a theology and a church that were patterned after it. Is there any possibility that they would conclude upon a doctrine and an organization that resembled anything known to the modern Bible-believing world? Unbiased and untutored readers of the holy book could never do it! The Bible could be read from now until doomsday without the concept of the Trinity occurring to any of its readers. Nor could we reasonably suppose that the doctrine of salvation by grace alone would somehow surface to float on top of the ocean of texts that demand obedience to the laws and ordinances of the gospel.

Only by some form of preconditioning can Bible readers be induced to ignore the countless passages that contradict the doctrine of the Trinity or the notion of salvation by grace alone. Both doctrines have an important history that stands independent of the Bible. A sympathetic view of that history is necessary to sustain either doctrine; the Bible alone simply does not do it. And what of Mormonism? Could we expect our unbiased and untutored readers to finish their reading of the Bible and then start the construction of temples, the practice of eternal marriage, and the sealing of families? I hardly think so. Again, the legitimacy of those doctrines stands independent of the Bible.

The Bible has no shortage of zealous defenders, indeed, countless souls profess loyalty to it. Yet their professions differ sharply. The differences are in the predetermined positions from which those holding these various views approach the book. Both Jew and Christian claim a reverence for the Old Testament and read it faithfully. But to read the Old Testament with the knowledge of the New Testament is to read with a different understanding and purpose. This knowledge shifts the book's center of gravity. Critics of Mormonism tell us that we are reading the Book of Mormon into the Bible. Well, of course we do. That is just what we are supposed to do. It would be faithless to do otherwise. Our Christian critics need to be reminded that they do the same thing with the Old Testament. Their faith demands it.

The common ground between Catholics, Protestants, and Jews should be the Hebrew Bible. If there is any hope of reconciliation among religions it should be found there. The arrangement of books, however, is very different in Christian and Jewish Bibles. The Christian order is based on the Septuagint, which the Jews have rejected. The Jewish Bible begins with the Pentateuch (the five books of Moses) followed by Joshua, Judges, Samuel, and Kings. Then come Isaiah, Jeremiah, Ezekiel, and the twelve Minor Prophets. They are followed in turn by the Writings (Psalms, Proverbs, and Job), the Scrolls (Song of Songs, Ruth, Lamentations, Ecclesiastes, and Esther), then Daniel, Ezra, and Nehemiah, and finally Chronicles.

This ordering conveys a distinct message. The book divides itself into two parts. The first is the story of the fall of Israel. This sad story recounts how the chosen people lost their chief city, their temple, and their land. It is the story of the rebellion and fall of Israel. It tells the story of the creation and fall of Adam and then the story of the creation of the nation of Israel and its fall to Babylon. The second half of the book is the story of Israel's return to the glory of David's day. The second half has been described as a "Quasi-legal brief on behalf of Israel and its claim to the land. The contention is that even though the original grant of land to them was conditional-provisional—and they failed to maintain the conditions—they didn't fulfill the requirements of the covenant and they lost the land. Nevertheless, overriding this historical truth is the original commitment made by God to Abraham in Genesis 15 (and repeated elsewhere to Abraham and his descendants)." Thus, this line of reasoning continues, "God committed himself by oath to give the land to Abraham and his descendants. According to their understanding, even if they deserved to lose it and lost it, they still have his claim because the original commitment was unconditional, irrevocable— 'To your offspring, I give this land' [Genesis 15:18]—and there's no way it can be reversed."[13]

The point here is that no one is willing to read the Common Bible (the Old Testament books that most Bible believers hold in common) from a neutral point of view. No one is reading those books to determine truth; for its readers the truth has already been determined. For traditional Christianity, it is the testimony of Christ; for the Jews, it is the claim to their ancient birthright; and far too often for the Latter-day Saint, it has been to prove the authenticity of the Book of Mormon. Everyone wants to suppose that the Bible is the key to truth when in reality its primary use has been as a sword to defend what has already been determined to be the truth.

The predetermined position from which a Latter-day Saint reads the Bible is that God can still speak, that revelation is continuous, that God can still call prophets, and that it takes modern revelation to give the true meaning to the ancient revelation, just as it takes the New Testament to give the true meaning to the Old Testament. If we are right, we are the only people on earth who truly understand the Bible.

The real issue is not the Bible itself; it is the a priori position from which it is read. In the world of biblical scholarship, study begins with the predetermination that there neither were nor are miracles. It is assumed that all references to them are unauthentic additions to the text. Could it surprise anyone that the conclusion of these same scholars is that Jesus is not divine, that he made no claim to Messiahship, to being the Son of God, the light of the world, or the bread of life?[14] That which people see and hear from the good book is largely determined by what they have conditioned themselves to expect.

Myth VII

TO KNOW THE BIBLE IS TO UNDERSTAND IT

Very few people really understand the Bible. There are appreciably more who have committed to memory a chain of passages from it that can be made to appear to sustain their dogmas, along with other texts they use to disprove the tenets of those with whom they disagree. Virtually without exception those so doing have no meaningful understanding of scripture or the gospel, and an honest examination of their arguments plays havoc with the fabric of both the immediate source they are quoting and the Bible as a whole.

Paul is perhaps the most misquoted man in earth's history; he is used endlessly in Christian evangelizing. He did not, however, write for that purpose. His epistles were all written to established congregations of believers. That is important because we have no business preaching grace to people who do not understand the nature of the Fall, nor do we sensibly teach mercy to someone who does not understand the necessity of divine justice. Such principles cannot be taught to someone who has not heard that God requires obedience and punishes disobedience. There are no scriptural texts that exhort sinners to "accept Christ," to "make a decision for Christ," to "ask Jesus into their heart," or to "accept Jesus as their personal Savior." Such invitations violate both the spirit and the terminology of the summons given by those Christ commissioned in the New Testament. The twentieth-century invitation "to make a commitment for Christ" is a far cry from the doctrine of the New Testament. Singularly, the word *commitment* is not used in the Bible. Christ and his disciples were a "covenant people," not a "commitment people." The difference is immense. Gospel covenants are made with God. They presuppose the principle of revelation, of a living priesthood, and that all the terms of salvation originate in the heavens. Commitments are individually determined. They require no revelation, no priesthood, and suppose that the terms of salvation are negotiable.

Further, many Bible readers have felt free to lay claim to the promises made within the holy book to others. Significantly, they have not felt the same disposition to claim the promised cursing that follows disobedience and broken covenants. In like manner, they suppose the commission to preach given to the ancient Saints somehow belongs to them while such injunctions as taking no thought for the morrow or giving all that they have to the poor remain unnoticed by them. This pick-and-choose theology bears little resemblance to the gospel taught by any of the Lord's chosen spokesmen in the Bible.

Myth VIII

THE BIBLE IS COMMON GROUND IN MISSIONARY WORK

For generations Latter-day Saints have attempted to prove the message of the Restoration to other Christian people by using proof texts from the Bible. The assumption sustaining those efforts is that the Bible is common ground. In reality, the Bible is not common ground; it is a battleground and has been for hundreds of years. Thus such efforts frequently result in a spirit of contention, generating more heat than light. Even when successful, such efforts are of questionable value. The testimony that leads to the waters of baptism must center in the reality that God speaks today, that Joseph Smith is a prophet, that the Book of Mormon is true, and that the Quorum of the Twelve Apostles and the First Presidency are Christ's rightful successors. Such a testimony cannot be sustained from biblical proof texts. A true testimony must embrace faith in the Bible, but it cannot rest on the Bible. For it to be otherwise would be unbiblical, for as we have already noted, the faithful Saints of whom we read in the Bible had no Bible. What they had was a faith founded on personal revelation. That faith was in harmony with and sustained by whatever scriptural texts were available to them, but it was not founded on them.

Like wolves, false notions travel in packs. The idea that we should prove the revelations of the Restoration from the Bible is a companion to the idea that we advance our cause by seeking common ground with those we seek to convert. It is as if we were saying, "Look, we are just like you are," and then acting surprised when our investigators say,

"Well, there is no need for me to change then, is there?" If we succeed in convincing people that our faith is the same as theirs, we have simply convinced them that our message is unnecessary.

What is particularly significant in this whole discussion is that it is easier to convert people to the Book of Mormon than it is to convince them of the truths of the Bible. If we convert people to the Book of Mormon, the truths of the Bible will become evident to them. If we convince them of the truths of the Bible, we are still left with the task of converting them to the Book of Mormon. The Lord told Joseph Smith that he gave us the Book of Mormon "to prove" the Bible true, not the other way around (see D&C 20:9–12). Joseph of Egypt was promised that a choice seer would come from his loins in the last days, one who would not only bring forth the word of the Lord but do a work that would cause the world to believe that portion of his word which they already had. Thus one of the great purposes of the Book of Mormon is to convince people that the Bible is true (see 2 Nephi 3:11; JST Genesis 50:30). To truly understand the Bible is to understand the necessity of continuous revelation.

Joseph Smith, in telling his own story of how he was able to obtain the mind and will of heaven, learned that "the teachers of religion of the different sects understood the same passages of scripture so differently as to destroy all confidence in settling the question by an appeal to the Bible." Had Joseph not chosen to drink from the fountainhead, we would still be lost in the "war of words and tumult of opinions" relative to the true meaning of the Bible (Joseph Smith–History 1:10, 12). We would, I suppose, still be awaiting what we know as the First Vision and the attendant restoration of the gospel.

NOTES

1. The Jews combine the twelve Minor Prophets into one book. They also combine 1 and 2 Samuel, 1 and 2 Kings, 1 and 2 Chronicles, and Ezra and Nehemiah.

2. F. W. Farrar, *The Bible: Its Meaning and Supremacy* (New York: Longmans, Green, and Co., 1897), p. 34.

3. See Williston Walker, Richard A. Norris, David W. Lotz, and Robert T. Handy, *A History of the Christian Church* (New York: Charles Scribner's Sons, 1985), pp. 67–69.

4. Walker, et al., *History of the Christian Church,* pp. 71–72.

5. Brigham Young, in *Journal of Discourses,* 26 vols. (London: Latter-day Saints' Book Depot, 1854–86), 14:280.

6. Floyd McElveen, *God's Word, Final, Infallible, and Forever* (n. p., 1985), pp. 139–42.

7. Another illustration would be the New English Bible, which reads: "For this people's mind has become gross . . ."

8. In verse 9 Jude is telling a story not found in the Old Testament text as it has come to us, but it was available to him and he obviously regarded it as scripture. He does the same thing in verses 14 and 15, this time quoting from an Enoch manuscript.

9. See *The Westminster Confession of Faith* (Inverness, Scotland: John G. Eccles Printers, Ltd., 1983), chap. 1, sec. 6, p. 22.

10. Joseph Smith, *Teachings of the Prophet Joseph Smith,* sel. Joseph Fielding Smith (Salt Lake City: Deseret Book, 1974), p. 61).

11. *Westminster Confession of Faith,* chap. 1, sec. 10, p. 24.

12. John Henry Cardinal Newman, *An Essay on the Development of Christian Doctrine* (Notre Dame, Indiana: University of Notre Dame Press, 1989), pp. 342–44.

13. David Noel Freedman, "How the Hebrew Bible and the Christian Old Testament Differ," *Bible Review* 9 (December 1993): 36–37.

14. See Marcus J. Borg, "Jesus in Four Colors," *Biblical Review* 9 (December 1993): 10.

Chapter Four

VANITY AND UNBELIEF

And your minds in times past have been darkened because of unbelief, and because you have treated lightly the things you have received—

Which vanity and unbelief have brought the whole church under condemnation.

And this condemnation resteth upon the children of Zion, even all.

And they shall remain under this condemnation until they repent and remember the new covenant, even the Book of Mormon and the former commandments which I have given them, not only to say, but to do according to that which I have written—

That they may bring forth fruit meet for their Father's kingdom; otherwise there remaineth a scourge and judgment to be poured out upon the children of Zion.

—Doctrine and Covenants 84:54–58

EMBARRASSMENT IS OFTEN a very effective teacher. One of my lessons centered on a Christmas gift from my parents. I had been away at college, and when I got home, Dad asked if there was something I wanted for Christmas. I told him that I would like to have the seven-volume set of the *History of the Church*. On Christmas morning I received those volumes. Nevertheless, my initial reaction was one of disappointment. I had not been given a new set, as I had anticipated, but an old, worn one. In fact, those books had been around much longer than I had. My grandfather had given them to my father years before when he had moved out of the old family home into an apartment and no longer had room for all his books. The second volume was partially covered with white paint, a reminder of the hurry with which we had built and painted a bookshelf to house Dad's new library. I didn't say anything about my disappointment with my hand-me-down books, but I must have been wearing it on my face because I heard my father say to my mother, "Well, Joseph seems disappointed." With the passing of the years I have come to regard those books as a special treasure. More than a few people would think it a privilege to own a set of books that had in turn been owned and used by both their father and their grandfather. The embarrassment associated with that memory has caused me to reflect. Just how often have we taken lightly the most sacred of treasures that we have been given and thus failed to accrue the blessings associated with them?

A PEOPLE UNDER CONDEMNATION

As part of a great revelation on priesthood given in September 1832, the Lord said of the infant Church, "Your minds in times past have been darkened because of unbelief, and because you have treated lightly the things you have received" (D&C 84:54). Let us consider what the Saints had received. For the first time in nearly eighteen hundred years, the heavens had been rent and revelation had commenced to flow from the royal courts on high. The priesthood of Aaron, with the attendant right to entertain angels and the authority to baptize for the remission of sins, had been restored to

Joseph Smith and Oliver Cowdery by John the Baptist himself. Within weeks of that event, the heavens were opened again, and Peter, James, and John appeared to Joseph and Oliver to confer upon them the priesthood of Melchizedek and its keys. This restoration of priesthood authority included the key of the knowledge of God, meaning the power and authority by which men in the flesh could stand in the divine presence and be tutored as were the prophets of old. It also included the authority by which the ancient apostles taught the gospel, presided over the Church, and unlocked the mysteries of heaven. Simultaneously with these nearly peerless events, Joseph and Oliver had been translating the Book of Mormon, a record of the dealings of God with the ancient inhabitants of the American continent, which record had also been received at the hands of an angel. Other revelations had flowed from heaven relative to the organization of the Church and the kingdom of God again on the earth and the restoration of all the knowledge, keys, and power ever enjoyed by any of the ancient Saints. By the time this revelation was given, eighty-five of the revelations in the Doctrine and Covenants had been received.

Never in earth's history had so many marvelous and miraculous things happened in so short a time. So much was happening so fast there can be little wonder that the Lord found it necessary to warn the Saints not to take lightly the deluge of spiritual power and knowledge that was being poured out upon them. To treat lightly events of such magnitude could only cause the powers of heaven to withdraw; and so it is that we hear the voice of the Lord saying that their "vanity and unbelief" had "brought the whole church under condemnation" (see D&C 84:55). As all were to share the blessings of heaven's light, so all must weather the storm of heaven's displeasure. The condemnation was to rest on all and was to remain until they repented and remembered "the new covenant, even the Book of Mormon and the former commandments," meaning the deluge of revelations they had received. These were to constitute the basis of their preaching and the standard by which they were to live. Only in following such a course could they "bring forth fruit" worthy of their Father's kingdom. Failure to appreciate what they had received would not only offend the heavens but demean the faith and courageous labors of the faithful in ages past, for they had longed to see that great day of restoration taking place. Such indifference, the Lord warned, would bring "a scourge and judgment" upon them. It would "pollute" the Lord's holy land, for this was a land that had been consecrated and set apart by prophets of old for the building of Zion in the last days (see D&C 84:56–59). It was a land that had been preserved by the hand of the Lord for that very purpose (see 2 Nephi 1:5). It was a land that had been redeemed by the shedding of blood, even the blood of their own noble forebears (see D&C 101:80).

Thus God in his mercy and patience said, "Verily, verily, I say unto you who now hear my words, which are my voice, blessed are ye inasmuch as you receive these things; for I will forgive you of your sins with this commandment—that you remain steadfast in your minds in solemnity and the spirit of prayer, in bearing testimony to all the world of those things which are communicated unto you." Then came the charge to go into all the world carrying the testimony of the marvelous work and wonder that had been wrought, even as the meridian apostles had done before them (D&C 84:60–61).

"MY WORD THROUGH YOU"

The revelations of the Restoration are both plain and emphatic about the message that we as a people have been charged to declare to the world. In what we know as the Lord's preface to the Doctrine and Covenants, we are told that he spoke to Joseph Smith from heaven and gave him commandments and that these commandments were in turn to be announced to all the children of men. The words of a living God were to be heralded again among men even as they had been anciently! The significance of such a thing is overwhelming. In an earlier revelation the Lord had said: "Thou shalt preach the fulness of my gospel, *which I have sent forth in these last days,* the covenant which I have sent forth to recover my people, which are of the house of Israel" (D&C 39:11; emphasis added).

Those commandments, or the "fulness of his gospel," as the Lord described them, were to be "proclaimed by the weak and the simple" even "before kings and rulers" (D&C 1:23). In an earlier revelation, the Lord had said, "I call upon the weak things of the world, those who are unlearned and despised, to thrash the nations by the power of my Spirit; and their arm shall be my arm, and I will be their shield and their buckler; and I will gird up their loins, and they shall fight manfully for me; and their enemies shall be under their feet; and I will let fall the sword in their behalf, and by the fire of mine indignation will I preserve them." The Lord then confirmed that he had "sent forth the fulness" of his gospel by the hand of Joseph Smith and "in weakness have I blessed him . . . . And I have given unto him the keys of the mystery of those things which have been sealed, even things which were from the foundation of the world, and the things which shall come from this time until the time of my coming" (D&C 35:13–14, 17–18). In a subsequent revelation, the Lord told Joseph Smith that he had been raised up so that the Lord might show forth his "wisdom through the weak things of the earth" (D&C 124:1).

"The weak and the simple," the Lord said, were to declare the fulness of his gospel (D&C 1:23). And that fulness was to be found in the Book of Mormon (D&C 20:9), which in turn constituted "the foundation of his church," which church, he said, was to come "forth out of obscurity and out of darkness, the only true and living church upon the face of the whole earth" (D&C 1:30).

In March 1829, while Joseph Smith was laboring with the translation of the Book of Mormon, the Lord told him, "This generation shall have my word through you" (D&C 5:10). That principle is profoundly significant. All who receive the gospel must receive it from those whom the Lord appoints in their own age and generation to declare it. We can read about the baptisms performed by John the Baptist countless times, but such reading will never remit our sins, nor will it give us the authority to baptize or the right to preach the gospel he taught. If it is a remission of sins we seek, we must seek it at the hands of a living administrator. The authority to preach baptism or to baptize must in like manner trace itself to one who held it, and had the keys, or the right, to give that authority to others.

When Christ commenced his mortal ministry, the ordinances of salvation ceased to be available through the law of Moses. For fifteen hundred years, the law of Moses was the only system on earth that had been ordained of God to teach his gospel and perform the ordinances of salvation. With the coming of Christ, salvation could no longer be found in the law of Sinai. Indeed, loyalty to that law demanded that its adherents leave it and embrace Christ, who was the living Law. After Christ had placed the twelve apostles at the head of his earthly Church and ascended into heaven, they became the conduits of the doctrines and covenants of salvation to all people, as Moses had been before them. So it remained until the day in which the apostles were taken.

In Adam's day, salvation was ministered through him, for he received the priesthood and its keys from the Creator[1] and had been taught the doctrines of salvation by angels sent from the presence of the Lord (see Moses 5:58–59). To reject Adam was to reject the authority and gospel that had been given him. That principle extends itself to all gospel dispensations. Those of each dispensation have been required to accept the message of salvation at the hands of prophets called from among their own number. A living church does not have dead prophets at its head. Those of Moses' day could not be saved by professing allegiance to Abraham, and those of Abraham's day could not be saved by professing allegiance to those of Noah's day. Thus, when the Lord told Joseph Smith that his generation (meaning dispensation) was to receive the word of the Lord through him, it was tantamount to saying that the hope of salvation could no longer be rooted in the words or authority of earlier prophets. Such instruction does not justify ignorance or neglect of the testimony of the earlier prophets; it simply places the voice of living prophets at the head. The faithful of all gospel dispensations have found salvation in and through the law of the gospel as that gospel was ministered to them by a living oracle.

We see this truth evidenced in the Book of Mormon when the nation of the Nephites at the time of Christ were all required to be baptized, notwithstanding that many, if not all, of them had been baptized previously (see 3 Nephi 11:21). Indeed, the only way we can be loyal to the prophets of ages past is to sustain the prophet called to stand at the head of our own dispensation and his lawful successors. Our profession to accept Christ is found in our willingness to accept those whom he sends to us. The covenant associated with the Melchizedek Priesthood is that those who hold the priesthood will sustain those called to preside over them, not those called to preside over another people in another time (see D&C 84:36).

Christ came not to destroy the law of Moses but to fulfill it. In like manner, the restoration of the gospel in our dispensation in no way nullifies the power or glories of the gospel in any past dispensation. Rather, it fulfills the promises made to the faithful of those dispensations. We reverence the teachings of their prophets; but when we go to general conference we sustain living prophets, seers, and revelators, not those sent to others in times past. As long as the church is the Lord's, it will be guided by his living voice, not by a distant echo from the hills of Judea.

WE MUST TEACH THE GOSPEL REVEALED TO US

We must teach the gospel as it was given to us. John the Revelator, who foresaw our day, said, "I saw another angel fly in the midst of heaven, having the everlasting gospel to preach unto them that dwell on the earth, and to every nation, and kindred, and tongue, and people, saying with a loud voice, Fear God, and give glory to him; for the hour of his judgment is come: and worship him that made heaven, and earth, and the sea, and the fountains of waters" (Revelation 14:6–7). After that angel had come and that gospel had been restored, Joseph Smith received the following revelation: "And now, verily saith the Lord, that these things might be known among you, O inhabitants of the earth, I have sent forth mine angel flying through the midst of heaven, having the everlasting gospel, who hath appeared unto some and hath committed it unto man, who shall appear unto many that dwell on the earth. And this gospel shall be preached unto every nation, and kindred, and tongue, and people" (D&C 133:36–37). This revelation confirms that the long promised restoration of the "everlasting gospel" had taken place and that the gospel restored by that angel was to go to all the nations of the earth. Moroni did not come to Joseph Smith and tell him that it was the duty of the elders to take the Bible to all the world. Rather, he told him that the Book of Mormon was to go to all the world, for it is the Book of Mormon that is destined to gather Israel.

How is it that we speak of the importance of the living voice on the one hand and the gathering of Israel through the testimony of ancient prophets on the other? It is the obligation of those of every gospel dispensation to declare those things revealed from the heavens to their dispensation. Though the Book of Mormon is the testimony of ancient prophets, it is a book written to people of our day; it is not a record known to the ancients. The first person to read it, other than those who wrote or compiled it, was the Prophet Joseph

Smith. He is the spokesman for Mormon spoken of by Lehi (2 Nephi 3:18).[2] By contrast, the Gospels and Epistles that compose the New Testament were directed to the people of the meridian dispensation.

THE MEASURE OF SPIRITUAL STABILITY

April 6, 1830, was designated by revelation as the day upon which the Church was to be organized (D&C 20:1–4). On that day, a revelation was given describing the role of the prophet and the relationship of the members of the Church to him. They were directed to "give heed unto all his words and commandments," which the prophet received from the Lord. His word, we are told, is to be received as if it came from the mouth of the Lord (see D&C 21:5). Those who so receive it are promised that the "gates of hell" shall not prevail against them, and that the Lord will "disperse the powers of darkness" from before them, "and cause the heavens to shake" for their "good, and his name's glory" (D&C 21:6). In addition, the Lord said that he would bless all those who labored in his vineyard with "a mighty blessing" for their faith on the words of Joseph Smith, which were given him by the Comforter (see D&C 21:9). This statement, Elder Bruce R. McConkie declared, constitutes the test of discipleship. The measure of one's spiritual stability, he said, lies in "how totally and completely and fully we believe the word that was revealed through Joseph Smith, and how effectively we echo or proclaim that word to the world."[3]

ORDINANCES AND DOCTRINES
MUST COME FROM THE SAME SOURCE

No one in the Church would claim validity for a priesthood ordinance that was not performed by the authority restored to Joseph Smith and Oliver Cowdery. Yet many have the idea that they can bypass the revelations of the Restoration in preference to those of the Bible in teaching the need for these same ordinances. The question that must be asked is, Can we get our doctrines from a source different from the source from which we obtain our authority? And if the doctrine can be had from some other source, then why not the authority also? Surely our source cannot be important in one case and not in another.

The Lord told Joseph Smith that the priesthood is to "administer the gospel" (D&C 84:19). All doctrines must originate with the priesthood and must flow through its channels. For us to find evidence that baptisms were performed anciently does not give us the authority to teach the necessity of baptism today. If we are to possess the same faith enjoyed by the ancient Saints, we must obtain it in the same way they did. Our claim to authority must be the same as theirs, and theirs never stood independent of living oracles. The plain fact of the matter is that no one has a legitimate claim to the doctrines of salvation without the authority to perform the ordinances of salvation, and both must trace themselves directly to God. Either there are living prophets, men to whom God speaks and who trace their authority directly to him, or there is no valid claim to priesthood. If there is no valid claim to priesthood, there is no valid claim to the gospel, either.

For the first paper I wrote as a college student, I read widely in popular periodicals and confidently quoted from them. I worked hard on the paper and expected a good grade. To my disappointment the grade was barely passing, and that due to the mercy shown a freshman student. The critique of the paper emphasized the importance of my using primary, or original, sources. The lesson was a good one. You get a lot of muddy water when you drink downstream. That is especially true when you are dealing with the doctrines of salvation. In school, no one wants to prepare for an important test by using someone else's notes. Certainly no sane teacher wants to be held responsible for saying everything that finds its way into his students' notes. On matters that count, we want our sources to be reliable. Courts of law have found hearsay evidence to be the source of so much mischief that they simply refuse to admit it. Strangely, most people ignore this important lesson when it comes to the source of their faith. Women who wouldn't buy a tomato without squeezing it trust their hope of eternal life to whatever religious tradition happens to prevail in their neighborhood. Men who wouldn't think of buying a car without kicking its tires and test-driving it likewise trust their eternal life to the traditions of their fathers, even when they don't believe those traditions. When salvation is at stake, we ought to know that both the message and the messenger are reliable. That can be the case only when both trace their authority directly to God.

The restoration of the authority to perform the ordinance of baptism is a classic illustration of this principle. Briefly, the story is as follows. Joseph Smith and Oliver Cowdery were translating the Book of Mormon. In doing so they learned of the instruction that the Savior gave the Nephite nation relative to baptism. It was a simple matter for them to reason that the principles involved were eternal and that if baptism was of such importance then, it must be so now. What is significant in this story is that they did not assume from what they read that they had any right to practice the ordinance. The authority to baptize does not come from reading an ancient text, no matter how perfect the translation. What Joseph and Oliver did was find a secluded place in the wilderness along the banks of the Susquehanna River where they could inquire of the Lord about the matter. In response to that prayer, a messenger from heaven appeared. He introduced himself as John, the same that is called John the Baptist in the New Testament. Joseph and Oliver were instructed about baptism and received the authority to perform it directly from the heavens (see Joseph Smith–History 1:68–75). Now all who desire the blessing of that saving ordinance can receive it at the hands of someone who traces both their understanding of the ordinance and the authority to perform it directly to its original source.

As Latter-day Saints, we are not practicing the ordinance of baptism because we find it in the New Testament. Nor do we refuse to practice it because it is not found in the Old Testament. If all copies of both Testaments were to disappear from the face of the earth, we would still baptize. We would do so because a messenger from heaven came to us bringing both the charge to practice the ordinance and the authority to perform it. The source of our authority is as important as the source of our knowledge. That becomes more obvious when we consider why we practice baptism for the dead. Ask any returned missionary why we do so. He or she will immediately refer to 1 Corinthians 15:29. It reads: "Else what shall they do which are baptized for the dead, if the dead rise not at all? Why are they then baptized for the dead?" The question is, What does that have to do with it? Are we practicing baptism for the dead because we found some obscure passage in the book of Corinthians that suggests that the Corinthians for some unstated reason were practicing it? Is that the thread that must bear the weight of all the pain and effort associated with this practice and the building of temples? Are we going to reason that Mormonism is true because we had the good fortune to find two sentences in the Bible that everyone else overlooked? Are we also going to argue that finding them somehow commissions us to do whatever it was that the ancients were doing? If so, are we going to afford that same license to everyone else who lays claim to some long-forgotten passage of scripture?

We do not practice baptism for the dead because we found an ancient text that suggests someone else once did. We would still practice baptism for the dead if we didn't have Paul's obscure and much-debated reference to it. In declaring our message, we would do much better to identify the real reason: we baptize for the dead because God commanded us to (see D&C 124:29–36).

In presenting our message, the question is, What kind of an approach is most likely to be sustained by the witness of the Spirit? In this instance is it the announcement that we have found an obscure Bible passage to justify our doctrine? Or is it the fact that the God of heaven still speaks, that he spoke through a prophet, and that he gave us the direction to do so? If the latter is a more appropriate way to teach baptism for the dead, then is it not also a more appropriate way to teach about baptism for the living?

TRUSTING WHAT WE HAVE BEEN GIVEN

When John the Baptist came to restore the Aaronic Priesthood, he promised that the Melchizedek Priesthood would be restored shortly thereafter. Between those events, while Joseph and Oliver continued translating the Book of Mormon, a revelation was given in which Oliver was assured that the things which he was writing were true. "I have manifested unto you, by my Spirit in many instances, that the things which you have written are true; wherefore you know that they are true," said the Lord. "And if you know that they are true, behold, I give unto you a commandment, that you *rely upon the things which are written; for in them are all things written concerning the foundation of my church, my gospel and my rock.*" Thus Oliver was instructed that if he was to build up the Lord's church, he must do it "upon the foundation" of that gospel they were restoring in the Book of Mormon. Oliver was promised that by trusting in this restored gospel, the gates of hell would not prevail against him (D&C 18:2–5; emphasis added).

Also while the Book of Mormon was being translated, Hyrum Smith was instructed by the Lord to prepare himself to declare His word. "Study my word which hath gone forth among the children of men (meaning the Bible), and also study my word which shall come forth among the children of men, or that which is now translating, yea, until you have obtained all which I shall grant unto the children of men in this generation, and then shall all things be added thereto." Emphasizing the importance of the things revealed "in this generation," the Lord cautioned Hyrum to "deny not the spirit of revelation, nor the spirit of prophecy, for wo unto him that denieth these things; therefore, treasure up in your heart until the time which is in my wisdom that you shall go forth" (D&C 11:22, 25, 27). That instruction, the Lord said, applied to all who desire to declare his work.

Similar instruction was given after the organization of the Church, when the Lord again emphasized that those who represent him do so by the proper authority and with the proper message. "Obey the law which I shall give unto you," the Lord said (D&C 42:2). As to the matter of who could declare his gospel, he said: "Again I say unto you, that it shall not be given to any one to go forth to preach my gospel, or to build up my church, except he be ordained by some one who has authority, and it is known to the church that he has the authority and has been regularly ordained by the heads of the church" (D&C 42:11). As to the message they were to deliver, the Lord said: "And again, the elders, priests, and teachers of this church shall teach the principles of my gospel, which are in the Bible and the Book of Mormon, in the which is the fulness of the gospel. . . . And all this ye shall observe to do as I have commanded concerning your teaching, until the fulness of my scriptures is given [this being a reference to the Prophet's labors on what we now call the Joseph Smith Translation]. And as ye shall lift up your voices by the Comforter, ye shall speak and prophesy as seemeth me good" (D&C 42:12, 15–16). Both the revelation given to Hyrum Smith and the more general instruction given in the latter revelation affirm the Bible as a source of our gospel understanding, though they emphasize that its teaching should be viewed from the light of the restored gospel.

The faith of the Church embraces ancient revelation but is not founded on it. The constitution of the Church is the voice of the living prophet. Instructing the early missionaries, the Lord said: "You shall declare the things which have been revealed to my servant, Joseph Smith, Jun. You shall begin to preach from this time forth, yea, to reap in the field which is white already to be burned" (D&C 31:4). Again the Lord said: "I have sent forth the fulness of my gospel by the hand of my servant Joseph: and in weakness have I blessed him; and I have given unto him the keys of the mystery of those things which have been sealed, even things which were from the foundation of the world, and the things which shall come from this time until the time of my coming, if he abide in me, and if not, another will I plant in his stead" (D&C 35:17–18).

Those going forth with the gospel message were to go forth in power. "Ye are not sent forth to be taught, but to teach the children of men the things which I have put into your hands by the power of my Spirit; and ye are to be taught from on high. Sanctify yourselves and ye shall be endowed with power, that ye may give even as I have spoken" (D&C 43:15). That is, they were to teach the revelations the Lord had given them. In fact they were given a revelation by the Lord to read to the Shakers that addressed their peculiar beliefs. Elder Leman Copley, who had been one of their number, was told that he was to "reason with them," not according to that which he had received from them, but rather according to that which he would be taught by his brethren in the priesthood. "By so doing," the Lord said, "I will bless him, otherwise he shall not prosper" (D&C 49:4; see also headnote). We have every reason to suppose that this principle is fundamental to all missionary work.

BEING TRUE TO THE REVELATIONS OF THE RESTORATION

In January 1832, a conference of the Church was held at Amherst, Ohio. At that conference a revelation was given to counsel the elders who had been laboring as missionaries. Not unexpectedly, they had encountered considerable difficulty in their effort to declare the message of the Restoration. They were instructed by the Lord not to tarry or to be idle but rather to labor with their might—lifting up their voices "as with the sound of a trump, proclaiming the truth according to the revelations and commandments which," the Lord said, "I have given you." That which the Lord had given them was the Book of Mormon. They were also promised that if they would be faithful in declaring the message they had been given, they would "be laden with many sheaves, and crowned with honor, and glory, and immortality, and eternal life" (D&C 75:3–5).

One is not a true messenger save he is true to his message. Ours is the message of the Restoration. It began in a grove of trees in upstate New York where both the Father and the Son appeared to the youthful Joseph Smith. It involved the appearance of a host of angels, the restoring of the powers and authorities that were theirs, the restoring of ancient scriptural texts, and a flood of light from heaven in the form of modern revelation that surpasses anything known in any past dispensation of the gospel. As Latter-day Saints we make no profession to any priesthood, keys, powers, authority, ordinances, or doctrines that we borrowed from another people. We stand independent. Our testimony is of a universal apostasy from the faith known to the ancient Saints. All was lost, and all requires restoring; ours is the story of that restoration. All that we profess must bear the label "modern revelation." Joseph Smith said it well: "Take away the Book of Mormon and the revelations (meaning those revelations he had received) and where is our religion? We have none."[4]

Such is the message that we have been commissioned to take to all the earth. To be faithful in that labor brings with it the promise of honor, glory, immortality, and eternal life; conversely, failure to be true to that divine commission on account of vanity and unbelief places us under condemnation.

NOTES

1. Joseph Smith, *Teachings of the Prophet Joseph Smith,* sel. Joseph Fielding Smith (Salt Lake City: Deseret Book, 1974), p. 157.

2. See Bruce R. McConkie, *A New Witness for the Articles of Faith* (Salt Lake City: Deseret Book, 1985), pp. 422–27.

3. Bruce R. McConkie, "This Generation Shall Have My Word through You," *Hearken O Ye People* (Sandy, Utah: Randall Book, 1984), p. 7.

4. Joseph Smith, *History of The Church of Jesus Christ of Latter-day Saints,* 7 vols., 2d ed. rev., ed. B. H. Roberts (Salt Lake City: The Church of Jesus Christ of Latter-day Saints, 1932–51), 2:52.

Chapter Five

WE BELIEVE THE BIBLE

And again, the elders, priests and teachers of this church shall teach the principles of my gospel, which are in the Bible and the Book of Mormon, in the which is the fulness of the gospel.
    —Doctrine and Covenants 42:12

BELIEF IN THE BIBLE IS AN article of faith with Latter-day Saints. No one can be baptized into the Church who does not believe that the Bible contains the word of God. All members of the Church in good standing hold the Bible to be divinely inspired. When Joseph Smith was asked if Mormons believed the Bible, he responded, "If we do, we are the only people under heaven that does, for there are none of the religious sects of the day that do." Asked how the Latter-day Saints differed from other sects, he replied, "In that we believe the Bible, and all other sects profess to believe their interpretations of the Bible, and their creeds."[1]

WE BELIEVE THE PLAIN MEANING OF THE BOOK

In his *History of the State of Utah*, Hubert H. Bancroft thought it necessary to evaluate the faith of the Mormon pioneers who were the state's first settlers. In so doing he concludes that "Mormonism in its religious aspect is simply the acceptation of the bible, the whole of it, literally, and following it to its logical conclusions." Bancroft does not intend such a statement as a compliment. In his mind, the Christian world had advanced in civilization and in intelligence from the time when people actually believed in Bible stories dealing with the likes of Moses, Jonah, and Job and had "thrown aside as unseemly blood-sacrifice and burnt offerings, sins of uncleanness, the stoning of sabbath breakers, the killing in war of women, children, and prisoners, the condemnation of whole nations to perpetual bondage, and many other revolting customs of the half savage Israelites sanctioned by holy writ." This, he observes, the ancients "did of their own accord, not because they were so commanded," but rather "in spite of commandments." He saw the religious world's abandonment of Old Testament practices as an expression of higher intelligence and of their outgrowing "the cruder dogmas of the early ages." Turning his attention to the New Testament, he notes that in like manner, as an expression of a higher cultural refinement, the Christian world had discarded such practices as speaking in tongues, going forth to preach without purse or scrip, the laying on of hands for the healing of the sick, raising the dead, casting out devils, the performance of miracles, and so forth. "There will be further repudiations as time passes," he accurately predicted, "further ignoring of portions of the scriptures by orthodox sects, a further weeding out of the unnatural and irrational from things spiritual and worshipful."[2] For the Mormons, however, he held no such hope, for they had chosen to interpret the Bible literally.

To Mormons, he explains, the Bible is "the inspired record of God's dealings with men in the eastern hemisphere; the Book of Mormon is the inspired record of God's dealings with the ancient inhabitants of this continent; the book of Doctrine and Covenants of the Church of Jesus Christ of Latter-day Saints consists of revelations from God concerning the present dispensation to Joseph Smith, who was inspired to translate the Book of Mormon and organize the church of Christ anew. Joseph Smith to the present dispensation," he explains, "is as Moses was to Israel; there is no conflict, either in personages or books. The statements, assertions, promises, and prophecies of the books, and the precepts and practices of the personages, are accepted, all of them, and held to be the revealed will to man of one and the same God, whose will it is the duty and endeavor of his people to carry out in every particular to the best of their ability."[3] The great danger in Mormonism, as Bancroft saw it, is that loyalty to the plain reading of the Bible.

The classic illustration of the Latter-day Saints' literal reading of scripture, in contrast to the figurative interpretation placed on it by traditional Christianity, deals with the nature of God himself. From Genesis to Revelation the Bible depicts God as an anthropomorphic being, one who created man in his own image and likeness. Holy writ declares us to be his offspring and records God introducing Christ to us as his Beloved Son. Christ, in turn, never referred to God by any title other than Father. Similarly, the Apostle Paul commences thirteen of his fourteen epistles with the announcement that he represented God "our Father" and "Jesus Christ our Lord." He began the book of Hebrews a little differently; there Paul declares the Son of God to be in the express image and likeness of the person of his Father. Latter-day Saints accept such descriptions of God according to the plain, direct, and obvious meaning of the words. When God is spoken of as being our Father, we believe him to be such; when we are spoken of as his children, we believe ourselves to be such; and when we are told that Mary was the mother of the Christ child, we believe her to have been such.

We recognize that there is much in the scriptures that is figurative, but we do not believe that God has been represented to us in a mystical metaphor. We believe ourselves to be the offspring of God, who fathered our spirits. We also believe that Christ, the firstborn among all the spirit children of our Father, was born into this physical and temporal state with God as his Father. In so believing we stand alone among all who profess allegiance to the teachings of the Bible. Again, we read literally; others read figuratively.

In his masterful work on the hellenization of Christianity, Edwin Hatch tells us that the great battle of the second century was between those who asserted that revelation had ceased and the canon closed and those who argued for continuous revelation. The victory went to the closed canon. The great battle of the third century, he says, was between those who claimed that the scriptures were to be taken in their literal sense and those who claimed that they required a philosophical interpretation. The victory went to the philosophers.[4] The gospel taught by Christ and his apostles was simply remodeled to make it more attractive to the highly educated Greeks. For instance, the philosopher-theologian Clement of Alexandria labored to show that the original revelations of the Bible and Greek philosophy were both threads of the divine intended to be woven together. "Abraham represents faith," he said, "Sarah, wisdom; Hagar, pagan culture; and the fact that Sarah gives birth to her son after Hagar signifies the contribution of Greek learning to the progress of true wisdom."[5] Origen, another of the ante-Nicene Fathers, who wrote extensively to prove that God had neither body, parts, nor passions, said: "With regard to Scripture as a whole, we are disposed to admit that all of it has a spiritual significance, but not all of it has a literal significance, since in several places it can be seen that a literal sense is impossible."[6] The efforts of such men were to eliminate through allegorical interpretation "passages too crudely anthropomorphic in their representation of divinity, which disconcerted educated Greeks and encouraged the rejection of the Old Testament by Gnostics."[7] The scriptures are of little use, Origen explained, to those who understand them as they are written.[8]

Justo L. Gonzales in his work *The Story of Christianity* tells us that two means were used by the church in the early years after the death of the apostles to harmonize what the Bible taught about God with the classical Greek notion of the supreme being. Those means were the doctrine of the Logos and the allegorical interpretation of scripture. The Logos doctrine holds that Christ is not really the Son of God but rather a representation of the mind of God in human form. All scriptural references to Deity are thus deemed to be figurative, or allegorical. The "allegorical interpretation was fairly simple to apply," Gonzales tells us. "Wherever Scripture says something 'unworthy' of God—that is, something that is not worthy of the perfection of the supreme being—such words are not to be taken literally. Thus, for instance, if the Bible says that God walked in the garden, or that God spoke, one is to remember that an immutable being does not really walk or speak."[9] So it was that God was robbed of both form and speech.

BELIEF IN THE BIBLE REQUIRES BELIEF IN REVELATION

All the great doctrines of modern Christianity trace themselves back to the tradition that the Bible is to be interpreted in a mystical or allegorical sense. Christian orthodoxy demands that the Bible be read figuratively.[10] This so-called orthodoxy, born of philosophical speculations, replaced the simple faith declared by Christ and his disciples. Given this bent of mind, it does not matter how many hundreds or even thousands of passages of scripture declare God to be a personal being. All such statements, no matter how plain they may be, are simply brushed aside as metaphorical. To suppose that words mean what they say is thought to be simplistic and primitive.

This concept dramatizes the difficulty of our centering our proselyting efforts on the Bible. The plain meaning of words is neutralized by the declaration that they are simply metaphorical. Thus in our dialogues with people of other faiths, we often find that the same words and texts have very different meanings. Before the Bible can become a truly effective proselyting tool, we must find a way to take it back nearly two thousand years and redecide the figurative vs. literal issue. Indeed, we must also redecide the question about whether the heavens are open or sealed. Significantly, that is exactly what the Book of Mormon does! It comes to us as an independent scriptural record contemporary with much of the Bible. Its doctrines affirm that we are to trust the plain meaning of words, and its testimony about the necessity of continuous revelation is unmatched.

The honest truth-seeker can neither neglect nor reject the opportunity to increase his or her understanding. I enjoyed acquaintance with a man who was a devoted student and teacher of the Bible. In his retirement years the opportunity came to him of going on a tour of the Holy Land. He refused that experience, explaining that over the years he had created his own mental picture of the events of the Bible and he didn't want them unsettled or disturbed. This same man would have been greatly chagrined if one of his students, having read the Gospel of Mark, refused to read Matthew, Luke, and John, claiming that what he had read was sufficient and that he didn't want to read something else that might unsettle his perspective on things. Undoubtedly my friend would have attempted to explain to his student the importance of learning all he could about the Savior and that much may be learned from the other Gospel writers that cannot be found in the book of Mark. We could also assume that my friend would have some concern about why anyone would be anxious to find security in a partial understanding of the ministry and teachings of Christ. Could it be that additional understanding might require greater devotion or commitment, that it might require change or even repentance? Returning our thoughts to the teacher, what of his attitude in not wanting to know more of the physical setting in which Christ taught? Could a knowledge of those circumstances sharpen or even change in some instances his understanding of the purpose and meaning of certain texts? And is it not axiomatic that a teacher who ceases to be an eager student also ceases to be an inspiration to those he teaches?

As we struggle to gain a true perspective on what it means to believe in the Bible, we ask, Does a belief in the book of Mark require a belief in the books of Matthew, Luke, and John also? Does the true believer have the prerogative of choosing one or two of the Gospels and setting the others aside, claiming sufficiency in what he has chosen? If the answer is that we cannot pick and choose where the word of God is concerned, the question must be asked, Can we believe in the New Testament without believing in the Old Testament? Can we disregard what God said to those before the time of Christ and still lay claim to the title of honest truth-seekers? If acceptance of the word of God in one dispensation embraces the responsibility to accept that word in all dispensations, could we not say that to truly believe the Old Testament requires that we accept the truth of the New Testament?

Such was the way the Book of Mormon prophets reasoned. Nephi concluded his record by addressing himself to all the ends of the earth: "Hearken unto these words and believe in Christ; and if ye believe not in these words believe in Christ. And if ye shall believe in Christ ye will believe in these words, for they are the words of Christ, and he hath given them unto me; and they teach all men that they should do good" (2 Nephi 33:10). In like manner we find Mormon testifying that the Bible is true because he knows that the Book of Mormon is true. "For behold, this is written [the Book of Mormon] for the intent that ye may believe that [the Bible]; and if ye believe that [the Bible] ye will believe this [the Book of Mormon] also; and if ye believe this [the Book of Mormon] ye will know concerning your fathers, and also the marvelous works which were wrought by the power of God among them" (Mormon 7:9).

In teaching this principle Brigham Young said: "There is not that man that hears the sound of my voice this day, that can say that Jesus lives, whether he professes to be his disciple or not; and can say at the same time, that Joseph Smith was not a Prophet of the Lord.

"There is not that being that ever had the privilege of hearing the way of life and salvation set before him as it is written in the New Testament, and in the Book of Mormon, and in the Book of Doctrine and Covenants, by a Latter-day Saint, that can say that Jesus lives, that his Gospel is true; and at the same time say that Joseph Smith was not a Prophet of God. That is strong testimony, but it is true. No man can say that this book (laying his hand on the Bible) is true, is the word of the Lord, is the way, is the guide-board in the path, and a charter by which we may learn the will of God; and at the same time say, that the Book of Mormon is untrue; if he has had the privilege of reading it, or of hearing it read, and learning its doctrines. There is not that person on the face of the earth who has had the privilege of learning the Gospel of Jesus Christ from these two books, that can say that one is true, and the other is false. No Latter-day Saint, no man or woman, can say the Book of Mormon is true, and at the same time say that the Bible is untrue. If one be true, both are; and if one be false, both are false. If Jesus lives, and is the Savior of the world, Joseph Smith is a Prophet of God, and lives in the bosom of his father Abraham. Though they have killed his body, yet he lives and beholds the face of his Father in heaven; and his garments are pure as the angels that surround the throne of God; and no man on the earth can say that Jesus lives, and deny at the same time my assertion about the Prophet Joseph. This is my testimony, and it is strong."[11]

The true believer in Christ will not be found picking and choosing among the things Christ taught, nor will he be found insulating himself by declaring mental retirement in the fear that additional knowledge will unsettle his present understanding. Gospel understanding comes "line upon line, precept upon precept," and it is not the prerogative of the true believer to stop a few precepts short, declaring his understanding to be sufficient. When the Spirit by which revelation comes is lost, the Spirit by which it is understood is also lost (see 2 Nephi 28:27–30).

It is fundamental to the faith of the Latter-day Saints that to believe in the Bible is to believe in the necessity of continuous revelation. In the physical world all species of life reproduce in their own image and likeness. So it is in the realms of spiritual things: faith begets faith, righteousness begets righteousness, and revelation begets revelation. Could it possibly be otherwise? To believe otherwise is to suppose that gospel principles are self-destructive and that by living by them, God would cease to be God. Indeed, the simple truth is that belief in one revelation is but the preparation to believe another and yet another. For us the Bible is a marvelous evidence that God can and does speak and that he will speak to those of this day if they but choose to listen.

ASKING GOD

The God of Mormonism is a God who speaks, and thus one of the distinctive characteristics of our faith is that all are required to obtain a personal witness by the Spirit that the message is true. Members of the Church are expected to have their own gospel dispensation. That is not to say that John the Baptist, or Peter, James, and John must appear to them personally to restore priesthood or that all the revelations of this dispensation must be given to them again; but it is to say that each and every member of the Church is required—and this is a matter of commandment—to seek and obtain his own sure knowledge of the verity of this great latter-day work. For instance, in announcing the Book of Mormon to be true, we always read the promise in the last chapter of Moroni to those we are teaching. It states that if they will read, ponder, and pray, they will come to know by the power of the Holy Ghost that the Book of Mormon is true (Moroni 10:3–5). Everyone we bring into the Church comes in on the condition that such prayers have been asked and that an affirmative answer has been received.

I have frequently asked classes of returned missionaries if they ever met anyone who, while professing a belief in the Bible, could at the same time honestly say they had prayed to know if it was true. I have yet to receive an affirmative response to that question. Even Latter-day Saints who have prayed fervently to gain a testimony of the Book of Mormon or of the Joseph Smith story have never thought it necessary to pray about the Bible. The matter is rather ironic. Nearly two thousand years ago, a Jew named Saul on the road to Damascus had a remarkable visionary experience. The scriptural accounts of his experience are contradictory, and for that matter were not recorded until at least twenty-eight years after the event.[12] Nevertheless, the Bible-believing world (that is, the Christian portion of it) accepts the story without reservation. No other proof is necessary than the simple fact that the Bible says it. If we change the name from Saul to Joseph, the time from two thousand years ago to less than two hundred years ago, and the place from Damascus to Palmyra, somehow the story becomes incredible to professed Bible believers. Virtually every missionary has heard someone say, "I would join your church if it were not for the Joseph Smith story." You would never hear anyone say, "I would be a Christian and believe the Bible if it were not for the story of Saul on the road to Damascus."

At issue here is whether revelation can be had in modern times. That is the reason Joseph Smith said that the Latter-day Saints were the only people on the earth who believed in the Bible. Why? Because they are the only ones willing to believe it when it says, "Ask God." They are the only ones who believe that God can still speak. If you don't believe that he can still speak, you don't really believe the Bible.

Joseph Smith believed it. He tested it, and he found it to be true. Those who say, "I would join your Church if weren't for the part about Joseph Smith," ought to be reminded that if it weren't for Joseph Smith, there would be no church to join! We don't hear anyone say, "I would accept the Ten Commandments if it weren't for that part about Moses and Sinai," or, "I would accept the Sermon on the Mount if it weren't for the part about Jesus." Those who had the faith to listen to and follow Moses did so because they accepted the reality of miracles and revelation in their own time. So it was with Christ. He worked miracles and spoke by way of revelation. To follow him required the same faith necessary to follow Moses. Can it be any different in our day? To share the faith of those of whom we read in the Bible, must we not also be willing to accept contemporary prophets, revelation, and miracles? Surely the ancients would think so, and so did Joseph Smith.

A DIVINE COMMISSION TO DEFEND THE BIBLE

The Church of Jesus Christ of Latter-day Saints is founded on the principle of revelation. Christ is and must be the direct and immediate source of all authority and doctrines in the Church. If revelation were to cease, the Church would no longer be Christ's church. Of necessity the Church must always have a living prophet at its head. The prophet is to the Church as Moses was to the children of Israel (see D&C 107:91). He is the covenant spokesman and speaks to the whole Church for and in behalf of the Lord. No authority or doctrine within the Church stands independent of his voice, for his is the voice of God to his people (D&C 1:38).

In any instance in which the Church embraces as doctrine revelations given to another people at another time—for instance, those revelations that constitute the Bible—they must first be confirmed as the mind, will, and word of the Lord by direct revelation. That is, they become a revelation to us only if the Lord designates them to be such. Many in the world today profess the Koran to be the word of God. The Latter-day Saints do not. Were we to accept it as scripture, we must do so under the Lord's direction. In like manner, many in the Bible-believing world profess a belief in what is known as the Apocrypha; we do not. The Lord told the Prophet Joseph Smith that many things contained in it are true and that it is for the most part translated correctly, yet there are many things in it that are not true, for those fifteen intertestamental books have also been subject to interpolations "by the hands of men" (D&C 91:1–2). The attentive reader will be struck by the absence of the prophetic element. At the same time, we accept the Bible as being divinely inspired and have the Lord's confirmation that such is the case.

Though Joseph Smith grew up in a family in which faith in the Bible was a natural inheritance, the spiritual validity of the book was confirmed for him by Moroni, who in his first instruction to the youthful prophet quoted liberally from both the Old and the New Testaments.[13] The work of translating the Book of Mormon would also have confirmed this, as its prophets quoted frequently from the Brass Plates, which contained Old Testament writings from the time of Adam to the time of Jeremiah (1 Nephi 5:10–13). In his discourse to the Nephites, the resurrected Christ quoted from such sources as Deuteronomy, Isaiah, Habakkuk, and Malachi (see 3 Nephi 20–25).[14] In April 1830, when Joseph Smith received the revelation to organize the Church, he was told that one of the Lord's purposes in bringing forth the Book of Mormon was to prove that "the holy scriptures" (meaning the Bible) are true. Of the Book of Mormon, the revelation stated it had been translated by "power from on high," that it was originally written "by inspiration," and that it had been and would be "confirmed" by angels (D&C 20:8–11).

In an earlier revelation, speaking of the Book of Mormon, the Lord said that Joseph Smith "has translated the book, even that part which I have commanded him," and then he added, "and as your Lord and your God liveth it is true" (D&C 17:6). Stronger language could not be used. If God lives, the Book of Mormon is true. To prove the Book of Mormon untrue is to prove that God has ceased to exist. No equivalent statement can be found for the Bible (or any other scriptural work for that matter). Nevertheless, the truthfulness of the Bible is an important Book of Mormon doctrine. Not only does the Book of Mormon sustain the truthfulness of the Bible by frequently quoting from it but it also assures us that as originally written, the Bible "contained the fulness of the gospel of the Lord" and went forth from the hands of its original writers "in purity unto the Gentiles, according to the truth which is in God." It was, however, only after these sacred texts had been corrupted by the "great and abominable church" that they made their public debut. Much that was plain and precious was taken from them along with "many covenants of the Lord." Because of that tampering with the scriptures, "an exceeding great many do stumble" and Satan has gained "great power over them" (1 Nephi 13:24–29). Those events, Nephi tells us, would be the antecedents to the ministry of the great seer of the latter days. He, it was prophesied, would have power given him "to bring forth my word" and to convince them of the truthfulness of that word which they already had. As in the revelation directing the organization of the Church, we are being told that the Book of Mormon is coming forth in defense of the Bible: "Wherefore, the fruit of thy loins [Lehi's descendants] shall write; and the fruit of the loins of Judah shall write; and that which shall be written by the fruit of thy [Lehi's] loins, and also that which shall be written by the fruit of the loins of Judah, shall grow together, unto the confounding of false doctrines and laying down of contentions, and establishing peace among the fruit of thy loins, and bringing them to the knowledge of their fathers in the latter days, and also to the knowledge of my covenants, saith the Lord" (2 Nephi 3:12).

Quite generally, we as Latter-day Saints have not paid proper attention to such marvelously significant prophecies. For instance, for generations we have attempted to prove that the Book of Mormon is true by quoting biblical texts. Our chain of thought embraces Isaiah's prophecy about a marvelous work and wonder that is to come forth in the last days. In the prophecy recorded in 2 Nephi 27, Isaiah describes a sealed book that is taken to a learned man, who says he cannot read (translate) it. Then it is taken to the unlearned man, who by the gift and power of God brings forth that which causes the wisdom of the wise to perish (see Isaiah 29). Next we quote Ezekiel 37, which tells the story of how Ezekiel went among his people with two sticks, or writing tables. Upon the first he had written, "For Judah, and for the children of Israel his companions," and upon the other he had written, "For Joseph, the stick of Ephraim, and for all the house of Israel his companions." He then joined them together and held them in one hand. When the people asked the meaning of his demonstration, he described a future day when the writings of Judah and Joseph would be joined together for the purpose of gathering Israel, that she might become again one nation, with one God, having their lands and their temple restored to them. Two key passages are then quoted from the New Testament. First, we quote John 10:16, in which the Savior says he has other sheep that are not of that fold, sheep that must also be brought so that there can be one fold and one shepherd. This reference foreshadows his visit to those of the house of Israel on the American continent. Then we quote a passage from the book of Revelation, in which the promise is given that an angel will come to the earth in the last days to restore the everlasting gospel, that it might be preached to every nation, kindred, tongue, and people (Revelation 14:6–7). The angel we know to be Moroni and the everlasting gospel to be the truths found in the Book of Mormon.

Without question the honest truth-seeker ought to be deeply

impressed with the chain of thought illustrated by these passages of scripture—two witnesses from the Old Testament and two from the New. The difficulty, however, is that such an approach to declaring the message of the Restoration is opposite to what the Savior directed. Our instruction is to use the Book of Mormon to prove the Bible true, not the Bible to prove the Book of Mormon true. When this truth is pointed out, the usual response is, Well, the Bible is common ground—we need to begin our discussion on common ground.

In fact, as we have shown, the Bible is not common ground; it is battleground and has been from long before the time of Christ. What if, when the Lord directed the children of Israel to march from Sinai to the promised land, they had said, No, we think it would be better for us to go to Egypt because that's common ground. They would not then have ended up where they were supposed to be. They would simply have returned to their previous bondage. The point is that it is not common ground we are seeking; it is holy ground. If we want to stand on holy ground, we had better follow the instruction the Lord has given us. Bruce R. McConkie stated it well when he said, "It is easier to convert people to the Book of Mormon than it is to convince them of what the Bible is really saying."[15]

Why have those of the Bible-believing world not read the words of Isaiah, Ezekiel, the Savior, and the Revelator and found themselves saying, My goodness, these passages are speaking of the Book of Mormon—we had better get hold of the Mormon missionaries! And how do we as Latter-day Saints know with such confidence that we have interpreted those passages correctly? The answer is simple: revelation. It takes revelation to understand the full and proper meaning of any scriptural text. We are confident in professing the meanings of those texts because we have a revealed understanding of them, and were it not for that revealed understanding, we would probably not see any more in them than do our sectarian friends. We know what those texts mean because the Lord told us. And where did he tell us? In the Book of Mormon, of course! If we want to understand the Isaiah prophecy, we must read 2 Nephi 27. If we want to understand the Ezekiel prophecy, we must read 2 Nephi 3. If we want to understand the Savior's statement about his intent to visit other sheep, we must read 3 Nephi 15. If we want to understand the prophecy in Revelation 14 about an angel who is to come to the earth with a message for those of every nation, kindred, tongue, and people, we must simply pick up the Book of Mormon and start reading. If we need the matter stated more specifically, then we read Doctrine and Covenants 133:36–40.

The fundamental point is that to believe the Bible, one must believe in revelation, because that is what the Bible professes to be. The Latter-day Saints have no interest in being another of the squabbling sects of Christendom. Scriptural interpretations are endless. That was the lesson that led Joseph Smith to the Sacred Grove. After having read the invitation in the book of James to all who lack wisdom to ask of God, Joseph Smith said: "Never did any passage of scripture come with more power to the heart of man than this did at this time to mine. It seemed to enter with great force into every feeling of my heart. I reflected on it again and again, knowing that if any person needed wisdom from God, I did" (Joseph Smith–History 1:12).

In so saying, Joseph Smith is giving us a perfect description of the Spirit of revelation. In a sense that could be thought a greater revelation than the one he received in the Sacred Grove, because that was the revelation that got him there. That true religion can be had only by those willing to ask of God may be the most important revelation that any of us can receive, for all else must be built upon this principle. Illustrating that he had obtained that all-important understanding, Joseph continued, saying: "For how to act I did not know, and unless I could get more wisdom than I then had, I would never know; for the teachers of religion of the different sects understood the same passages of scripture so differently as to destroy all confidence in settling the question by an appeal to the Bible" (Joseph Smith–History 1:12).

ON BEING COMPETENT WITNESSES OF THE BIBLE

Most professing Bible believers have little or no real understanding of what the Bible is really about. They read with a blind eye, carefully choosing those bits and snatches that justify the course they have already determined to follow. They deny the Spirit of revelation and read by the light of the lamp of their own conceit. Of necessity the question must be asked, What constitutes a competent witness of Bible truths? Or by what standard do we determine which of the many voices interpreting the Bible we should give credence to?

To clarify our own position, let us simulate an interview between an honest truth-seeker and a Latter-day Saint who has a clear understanding of the significance of the message of the Restoration.

Truth-seeker: "Do Latter-day Saints accept the Bible as the word of God?"

Latter-day Saint: "We most certainly do."

Truth-seeker: "What gives you that confidence? How do you know that it represents the mind and will of Deity?"

Latter-day Saint: "Because our experience with the Bible is first-hand. We believe that there was a man Adam because the man Adam appeared to Joseph Smith and ministered to him. We believe in the reality of Noah because he too appeared to the Prophet. In like manner so did Moses, Elijah, John the Baptist, Peter, James, John and many others of whom we read in the Bible record (see D&C 2; 13; 110; 128). They were the Prophet's tutors. They instructed him and laid their hands upon his head and gave him the same keys, powers, and authorities by which they taught the gospel and performed its sacred ordinances. We believe in the Bible because we have associated with its chief characters and have been instructed and blessed by them."

Truth-seeker: "All that you are saying depends on the credibility of Joseph Smith. Isn't that a rather heavy burden to place on a single man?"

Latter-day Saint: "Joseph Smith was the recipient of many marvelous spiritual experiences, but in all those I have just mentioned, he was never alone. Whenever keys or authority were being conferred, someone else was with him. All such things can be sustained in the mouths of two witnesses. For instance, Joseph received much instruction from the angel Moroni, a prophet who had lived in the Americas about four hundred years after the resurrection of Christ. Joseph introduced Moroni to three of his closest friends, David Whitmer, Martin Harris, and Oliver Cowdery. We have their written testimony of the event."

Truth-seeker: "You mean to tell me that an angel appeared to Joseph Smith and that Joseph Smith in turn introduced that angel to three of his friends?"

Latter-day Saint: "That is exactly what I am telling you."

Truth-seeker: "Well, what about his revelations? Were they not received in private?"

Latter-day Saint: "I wouldn't want to say that he couldn't receive a revelation without others present, but that was generally not the case. Many of his revelations were received and recorded while he sat in council with his brethren or at conferences of the Church."

Truth-seeker: "You speak of the experiences of Joseph Smith as if they were your own. Does his competence as a witness make you a competent witness also?"

Latter-day Saint: "One is a competent witness only to the extent that one's experience is immediate and personal. I have not had personal association with the prophets of dispensations past, but I have experienced in a very personal way the blessings associated with the keys, powers, and authority they have restored. For instance, I have been instructed by apostles and prophets and have had them lay their hands on my head to give special blessings that have been fully realized. Because of that experience, I have no difficulty believing that people in Old and New Testament times shared the same kind of experience. I have witnessed healings, the operation of spiritual gifts, the spirit of revelation, and the performance of miracles. Indeed, I have on numerous occasions been personally involved in such experiences. Thus, I have no difficulty believing that such things were enjoyed by the ancient Saints as the holy scriptures attest."

Truth-seeker: "Are there any powers known to the ancients that are not a part of what you declare to be the restored gospel?"

Latter-day Saint: "None. Our knowledge is not bound in the covers of a book. It is found in the things we experience. We do not embrace the sectarian notion that our religion is Bible religion because the Bible is not religion—it is simply a history of those who had religion. True religion is a living thing, and our religion lives."

THE MEANING OF A GOSPEL DISPENSATION

Returning our attention to Doctrine and Covenants 20, the revelation that directed Joseph Smith to organize the Church, having announced that the Book of Mormon was given as evidence that the Bible is true, it also stated that it was given as evidence that God does call inspired men in our day and that he is the same yesterday, today, and forever. By these proofs, the revelation states, "shall the world be judged, even as many as shall hereafter come to a knowledge of this work." Those who receive it in faith and work righteousness are promised "a crown of eternal life," whereas those who reject it do so unto their own condemnation. Then we are told that it is "by these things" that we who have joined the Church "know that there is a

God in heaven" and come to a knowledge of all other saving principles of the gospel of Jesus Christ (vv. 11–28). This revelation lays the foundation upon which the Church is to be built. That foundation is faith in the reality of the First Vision and the Book of Mormon as containing "the fulness of the gospel of Jesus Christ" (v. 9). It is "by these things" that Latter-day Saints come to the knowledge "that there is a God in heaven" (v. 17) and obtain an understanding of all other saving principles (vv. 17–28). Thus the dispensation of the fulness of times was formally ushered in.

A gospel dispensation is a period of time in which all that is necessary for the salvation of men is dispensed from the heavens anew. Thus those of that dispensation stand independent of all previous dispensations, not in the sense that the truths of salvation have changed—for God is the same yesterday, today, and forever—but in the sense that they come to a knowledge of those truths by revelations that are unique to them.

Our message centers on the events that took place in the Sacred Grove. That is the story that we seek to tell. It is not common ground that we seek; it is holy ground. Our message does not center on the truth that God spoke in times past but rather that he has and does speak in our day. We honor the dead prophets by listening to the living prophets. We unfold the true meaning of the Bible only as we give heed to its living counterparts. The best possible defense for the truthfulness of the Bible is a people in our day possessing the same faith, having the same gifts and powers, and performing the same marvelous works as did their ancient counterparts. There is no better proof of the validity of ancient revelation than modern revelation.

NOTES

1. Joseph Smith, *Teachings of the Prophet Joseph Smith,* sel. Joseph Fielding Smith (Salt Lake City: Deseret Book, 1974), p. 120.

2. Hubert Howe Bancroft, *History of Utah* (San Francisco: The History Company Publishers, 1890], p. 333.

3. Bancroft, *History of Utah,* p. 334.

4. See Edwin Hatch, *The Influence of Greek Ideas on Christianity* (Gloucester, Mass., 1970), pp. 324–25.

5. Manlio Simonetti, *Biblical Interpretation in the Early Church,* trans. John A. Hughes (Edinburgh: T&T Clark, 1994), p. 38.

6. Simonetti, *Biblical Interpretation,* p. 45. For the original source, see *De Prince* 4.3.5.

7. Simonetti, *Biblical Interpretation,* pp. 45–46.

8. See Joseph Fielding McConkie, *Sons and Daughters of God: The Loss and Restoration of Our Divine Inheritance* (Salt Lake City: Bookcraft, 1994), p. 82.

9. Justo L. Gonzales, *The Story of Christianity,* 2 vols. (New York: Harper & Row, 1984), 1:160.

10. See John Henry Cardinal Newman, *An Essay on the Development of Christian Doctrine* (Notre Dame, Ind.: University of Notre Dame Press, 1989), p. 344.

11. Brigham Young, in *Journal of Discourses,* 26 vols. (London: Latter-day Saints' Book Depot, 1854–86), 1:38.

12. The book of Acts tells the story three times (Acts 9:2–7; 22:6–11; 26:12–18). Each account differs somewhat from the others. For instance, in the first we are told that those with Paul heard the voice from heaven but did not see the Lord. In the second we are told that they did not hear the voice. The third does not address that issue but announces that the Lord spoke to Paul in Hebrew.

13. A reconstruction of what Moroni told Joseph Smith includes references from Deuteronomy, Psalms, Isaiah, Jeremiah, Joel, and Malachi from the Old Testament. In the New Testament he quoted from Matthew, John, Acts, 1 Corinthians, and Thessalonians. See Joseph Fielding McConkie, *His Name Shall Be Joseph* (Salt Lake City: Hawkes, 1980), p. 58.

14. In 3 Nephi 21:9 the Savior is paraphrasing Habakkuk 1:5. In 3 Nephi 21:11 he is paraphrasing Moses' great prophecy recorded in Deuteronomy 18:18–19.

15. Personal conversation, 1983.

Chapter   Six

THE ARM OF THE LORD
REVEALED

And the arm of the Lord shall be revealed; and the day cometh that they who will not hear the voice of the Lord, neither the voice of his servants, neither give heed to the words of the prophets and apostles, shall be cut off from among the people.
                    —Doctrine and Covenants 1:14

AMONG THE PROPHETS whose words are preserved in the Bible, Isaiah is known as the great prophet of the Restoration. No one else wrote as explicitly, as completely, or with as great eloquence and power as he did of the events of the last days—events he described as "a marvellous work and a wonder" (see Isaiah 29:14). Among his prophetic promises we find these words: "The Lord hath made bare his holy arm in the eyes of all the nations; and all the ends of the earth shall see the salvation of our God" (Isaiah 52:10). In what day will the earth "see the salvation," meaning victory or triumph, of their God? In that day in which Israel will again have been gathered and the promises made to her ancient fathers fulfilled. Great battles will precede that day, battles in which it will be necessary for the Lord of Hosts, the Lord of Battles, to bare his arm as a warrior to bring victory to the army of Israel.

ISRAEL'S VICTORY WILL COME IN THE TEACHING OF THE GOSPEL

Nephi interprets Isaiah's prophecy of the Lord's making bare his holy arm in the context of fulfilling the promise of the Lord to Father Abraham. "In thy seed," the Lord told Abraham, "shall all the kindreds of the earth be blessed." Nephi reasons that all the kindreds of the earth cannot be blessed save "the Lord bare his arm" among them, that is, unless he brings "his covenants and his gospel unto those who are of the house of Israel" scattered among all the nations of the earth. Wherefore, he will bring them again out of captivity, and they shall be gathered together to the lands of their inheritance; and they shall be brought out of obscurity and out of darkness; and they shall know that the Lord is their Savior and their Redeemer, the Mighty One of Israel" (1 Nephi 22:9–12).

The word *arm* carries two common meanings: that of an appendage to the body and that of a weapon. Thus "to be armed" is to have a weapon, and a group of armed men is called an "army." For the Lord to make bare his arm among all people is for him to send forth an army of missionaries to declare his gospel with the covenants of salvation unto the ends of the earth. His victory is in the triumph of truth over darkness, in all men coming to know him as their Lord and their Savior. Living the principles of the gospel and keeping covenants bring great spiritual power to all who march under the Lord's banner. Of that vast army of missionaries he will send forth, the Lord has said: "And their arm shall be my arm, and I will be their shield and their buckler; and I will gird up their loins, and they shall fight manfully for me; and their enemies shall be under their feet; and I will let fall the sword in their behalf, and by the fire of mine indignation will I preserve them" (D&C 35:14).

"The voice of warning shall be unto all people," the Lord told the Prophet Joseph Smith, "by the mouths of my disciples, whom I have chosen in these last days." Further, the Prophet was assured, "The arm of the Lord shall be revealed; and the day cometh that they who will not hear the voice of the Lord, neither the voice of his servants, neither give heed to the words of the prophets and apostles, shall be cut off from among the people" (D&C 1:4, 14). The language of this revelation is similar to that spoken by the Savior to the Nephites as he foreshadowed these marvelous events: "It shall come to pass that whosoever will not believe in my words, who am Jesus Christ, which the Father shall cause him [Joseph Smith] to bring forth unto the Gentiles, and shall give unto him power that he shall bring them forth unto the Gentiles, (it shall be done even as Moses said) they shall be cut off from among my people who are of the covenant" (3 Nephi 21:11). I believe that is the single most important passage of scripture in the Book of Mormon. It binds God's covenant with Abraham to the testimony of Christ as found in that sacred volume. It means that none will be acknowledged as Abraham's seed without their having first accepted the prophetic role of Joseph Smith and the testimony of Christ as it is found in the Book of Mormon. It means that Joseph Smith, as the revealer of the Book of Mormon, stands at the head of the gathering of Israel.

The declaration by the Savior makes the patriarchal blessing given to the Prophet by his father, Joseph Smith Sr., most remarkable: "A marvelous work and a wonder has the Lord wrought by thy hand, even that which shall prepare the way for the remnants of this people to come in among the Gentiles, with their fulness, as the tribes of Israel are restored. I bless thee with the blessings of thy Fathers Abraham, Isaac and Jacob; and even the blessings of thy father Joseph, the son of Jacob. Behold, he looked after his posterity in the last days, when they should be scattered and driven by the Gentiles, and wept before the Lord; he sought diligently to know from whence the Son should come who should bring forth the word of the Lord, by which they might be enlightened, and brought back to the true fold, and his eyes beheld thee, my son; his heart rejoiced and his soul was satisfied and he said, As my blessings are to extend to the utmost bounds of the everlasting hills; as my father's blessings prevailed, over the blessings of his progenitors, and as my branches are to run over the wall, and my seed are to inherit the choice land whereon the Zion of God shall stand in the last days, from among my seed, scattered with the Gentiles, shall a choice Seer arise, whose bowels shall be a fountain of truth, whose loins shall be girded with the girdle of righteousness, whose hands shall be lifted with acceptance before the God of Jacob to turn away his anger from his anointed, whose heart shall mediate great wisdom, whose intelligence shall circumscribe and comprehend the deep things of God, and whose mouth shall utter the law of the just . . . and he shall feed upon the heritage of Jacob his father: Thou [Joseph Smith Jr.] shall hold the keys of this ministry, even the presidency of this Church, both in time and in eternity, and thou shalt stand on Mount Zion when the tribes of Jacob come shouting from the north, and with thy brethren, the Sons of Ephraim, crown them in the name of Jesus Christ."[1]

When Moroni appeared to the youthful Joseph Smith, he explained many passages of scripture that foreshadowed the latter-day gathering of Israel. Among the passages he quoted were the words of Peter, in which the New Testament apostle spoke of a time of restitution and of the time foreseen by Moses when the ancient lawgiver instructed his people: "A prophet shall the Lord your God raise up unto you of your brethren, like unto me; him shall ye hear in all things whatsoever he shall say unto you. And it shall come to pass, that every soul, which will not hear that prophet, shall be destroyed from among the people" (Acts 3:22–23). Moroni explained that the prophet referred to by Peter was Christ, but though the day had not yet come when "they who would not hear his voice should be cut off from among the people," it soon would come (see Joseph Smith–History 1:40).

KNOWLEDGE WITHOUT UNDERSTANDING

At the conclusion of a recent Book of Mormon course I was teaching for returned missionaries at Brigham Young University, a student observed that he had been taught in another class that there were no doctrines in the Book of Mormon that could not be found in the Bible. I could only hope that what he was saying did not accurately represent what his other teacher had said. Coincidentally, just before that class period I had been grading student essays on the topic "What do we learn in 3 Nephi from the Savior about our responsibility to accept him?" The last essay that I had read left me wondering if its author had bothered to read 3 Nephi or had been attending class, and, if so, how he had so completely filtered out every meaningful thing that had been taught. Those two experiences, standing within minutes of each other, along with the class discussion that followed the student's question, did much to convince me that despite our best efforts, both faculty and students have not really understood the importance of the testimony that the Book of Mormon bears of Christ or the real necessity of the latter-day restoration of the gospel.

It is easier to reassemble shattered glass than to reconstruct a class discussion, but let me attempt to identify some of the things that were said in class that day. To give some perspective to our discussion, I asked the class if they knew of any instance in which people had devoted themselves to serious study of the Old Testament and yet had missed its most important message. They struggled with the question but after a while it dawned on them that that was precisely what the Jews had done in Jesus' day. They had "the Law and the Prophets," the primary purpose of which was to prepare them to accept Christ. Paradoxically, not only did they reject Christ but they used those scriptures as their justification in so doing. From there we moved to the New Testament. I posed the same question. Could they identify any instance in which a people had intently studied it and yet missed the heart of its message? Again the class struggled. After all, they reasoned, the Christian world has accepted Christ. I asked if studying the New Testament had helped prepare people to accept their missionary message. Their answers were both affirmative and negative. Certainly such study had helped those who were honest in heart, but it was used by others as an excuse to reject the message of the Restoration. Their experience evidenced that just as many Jews had used the Old Testament to find justification to reject Christ, so too were many Christians using the New Testament to find justification to reject the restored gospel in our day.

Having established these two examples, the class was prepared to accept the possibility that people could also study the Book of Mormon and obtain a great deal of knowledge and information about it but still miss its central point. I suggested that we might profitably consider an appropriate response to the question in the essay they had been asked to write: "What do we learn in 3 Nephi from the Savior about our responsibility to accept him?" Our discussion centered on what I told them was the most important passage in all of the Book of Mormon, namely, 3 Nephi 21:11. The plain meaning of that text is that all in our dispensation must accept the testimony of Christ as it is found in the Book of Mormon or they cannot participate in the covenants of salvation and thus will be left, in the words of Malachi (which the Savior also quoted), without "root or branch," meaning family ties, in the world to come (see 3 Nephi 25:1).

The statement clearly makes acceptance of the Book of Mormon and its testimony of Christ a condition of salvation. The testimony that Jesus is the Christ because Matthew, Mark, Luke, and John so declare is no longer sufficient. The testimony of the Book of Mormon writers is established as the standard here. Why would that be the case? Don't we honor the testimony of the New Testament prophets? Of course we do. Yet one can profess to accept the testimony of the New Testament and believe whatever one wants relative to the plan of salvation. Only when one accepts the testimony of the Book of Mormon prophets does one accept the obligation to accept the divine mission of Joseph Smith and the message of the Restoration.

Some very significant Book of Mormon doctrines relative to Christ cannot be found in the Bible. For instance, consider the role of Christ in redeeming men from the effects of Adam's fall. One can read the Bible from Genesis to Revelation and not find a definition of the word *resurrection*. In fact, the word is not used in the Old Testament. By contrast the Book of Mormon makes it unmistakably plain that resurrection consists of the inseparable union of body and spirit (see Alma 11:45). An understanding that the plan of salvation requires a corporeal body is essential to understanding the full effects of Adam's fall and Christ's atonement. Lehi's son Jacob teaches us that because of the Fall, body and spirit separate in death, the body to "crumble to its mother earth, to rise no more" and the spirit that inhabited it to become subject to the devil. Jacob explains that "our spirits must have become like unto him, and we become devils, angels to a devil, to be shut out from the presence of our God, and to remain with the father of lies, in misery, like unto himself" throughout the endless eternities, save Christ had worked out his atoning sacrifice (see 2 Nephi 9:7–9). The body and the spirit have no power to reunite themselves. Because no unclean thing can enter the presence of God and because the spirit has no power to cleanse itself from sin, it would become subject to the author of sin and as such a citizen of the kingdom of darkness. Thus Lucifer would rule as king over all the dead in a kingdom that knows no light, no agency, and no freedom. All must, under such circumstances, worship him. Yet, as Father Lehi explained, the Messiah came to redeem the children of men from the Fall. "And because that they are redeemed from the fall they have become free forever, knowing good from evil; to act for themselves and not to be acted upon, save it be by the punishment of the law at the great and last day, according to the commandments which God hath given" (2 Nephi 2:26). Lehi is telling us that agency, freedom, and the ability to distinguish between good and evil exist only because of the atonement, or grace, of Christ. Without those three essential elements, there could be no plan for the salvation of mankind. Expanding this concept, Joseph Smith taught us that every principle of the gospel is an appendage to the atonement.[2] All saving principles exist because of the grace of Christ.

The Atonement, Jacob tells us, is infinite and eternal. Because of it, the twin monsters, death and hell, have no permanent hold over the souls of men. The grave must yield up every soul that it possesses, and every living thing is enabled to enjoy the inseparable union of body and spirit. From modern revelation we know that the glory of resurrected souls will differ according to the law they chose to obey. Some will come forth in a glory like unto that of the sun, others in a splendor like the moon, and still others in glory represented by the stars. These glories have been designated as celestial, terrestrial, and telestial (see D&C 88:20–32). As the atonement of Christ brought victory over the grave, so it brought victory over man's separation from the presence of God. All will be brought back to stand in the divine presence and there account for their works in the flesh. So it was that Christ came into the world that he might "save all men" if they would but "hearken unto his voice; for behold,

he suffereth the pains of all men, yea, the pains of every living crea-
ture, both men, women, and children, who belong to the family of
Adam. And he suffereth this that the resurrection might pass upon
all men, that all might stand before him at the great and judgment
day" (2 Nephi 9:21–22).

Through his atoning sacrifice Christ satisfied the demands of justice. Payment was made for the sins of all mankind. Thus, in so suffering, Jesus becomes more than our Savior. He also becomes our
Lord and Master, having bought us with the price of his blood.
Because of that infinite act of grace, he rightfully gives us commandments, which we may obey or disobey, according to the freedom and agency he has given us. Of those who choose the path of
obedience, Alma said, "These are they that are redeemed of the Lord;
yea, these are they that are taken out, that are delivered from that
endless night of darkness; and thus they stand or fall; for behold,
they are their own judges, whether to do good or do evil. Now the
decrees of God are unalterable; therefore, the way is prepared that
whosoever will may walk therein and be saved" (Alma 41:7–8). "And
thus mercy can satisfy the demands of justice, and encircles them in
the arms of safety," Amulek explained, "while he that exercises no
faith unto repentance is exposed to the whole law of the demands
of justice; therefore only unto him that has faith unto repentance is
brought about the great and eternal plan of redemption" (Alma
34:16).

With such concepts clearly in mind, we return to the statement
of the Savior in 3 Nephi 21:11 that all must accept the testimony of
him as it is found in the Book of Mormon. Much reverence for Christ
can be found in the Bible-believing world, but a knowledge of the
principles just rehearsed cannot be found. They simply are not there.
As marvelous as the Bible is in telling us the story of Christ's ministry, it does not, in its present state, clearly define resurrection so
that we know that it is the inseparable union of body and spirit. The

idea of a spirit world where disembodied spirits await the day of their resurrection is not a part of the theologies of traditional Christianity. The knowledge that had there been no atonement they would have remained in that spirit prison throughout the endless expanses of eternity, enslaved to their tyrant king, knowing no good, exercising no agency, and experiencing no joy, is not had among them. The fulness of his grace in redeeming us from both the grave and eternal bondage to the evil one is not had by them. Nor is an understanding of the eternal balance that must exist between the principles of mercy and justice. An understanding of those principles is necessary to understand that the grace of Christ does not negate but in fact creates the necessity for obedience to the laws and ordinances of the gospel whereby we can be saved. Thus we are freed from a false representation of Christ in theologies that append salvation to ritual performance, such as the receiving of certain sacraments, and the equally false notion that salvation is found in the suffering of Christ alone and our simple acknowledgment of it. The first doctrine creates the notion of deathbed repentance; the second, a lip-service religion. Neither represents the discipleship required of true believers.

As Latter-day Saints we may have failed to recognize the distinctive nature of the testimony we bear, but the world has not. To illustrate the point let me return to our class discussion. I asked the class members if they were called to return to the missions in which they had served (more than forty missions were represented in our class) but instead of testifying that Joseph Smith was a prophet and that the Book of Mormon was true they were asked to testify of Christ and the truthfulness of the Bible, would there be a difference in the reception they received? No discussion was necessary. Everyone agreed that to free themselves of the Joseph Smith story and the Book of Mormon would make them appreciably more acceptable to the world. Why the difference if both books contain the same message?

If the Book of Mormon was without the power to overturn the theologies of the world, it would go unopposed by them.

One cannot believe in the Book of Mormon without believing in the opening of the heavens and the role of living prophets. Those who accept the Book of Mormon, like those who accepted Christ during his mortal ministry, do so in opposition to the orthodoxy and traditions of the day. The similarity between accepting the mortal Christ and accepting the Book of Mormon is too striking to be anything other than by divine design.

RIGHTEOUSNESS AND TRUTH TO SWEEP THE EARTH

Enoch recorded a panoramic vision that reached from his day to the time when his city would return to the earth as part of Christ's millennial reign. The prophetic account given in that vision of our dispensation is most instructive. Of necessity it is very brief, almost terse, yet it is marvelously comprehensive. It begins with the litany of signs that are to be manifest in the heavens. "And the day shall come that the earth shall rest," it promises, "but before that day the heavens shall be darkened, and a veil of darkness shall cover the earth; and the heavens shall shake, and also the earth; and great tribulations shall be among the children of men, but my people will I preserve" (Moses 7:61). Then in broad sweeping strokes Enoch's vision depicts the great events to be associated with the dispensation of the fulness of times. "And righteousness will I send down out of heaven; and truth will I send forth out of the earth, to bear testimony of mine Only Begotten; his resurrection from the dead; yea, and also the resurrection of all men; and righteousness and truth will I cause to sweep the earth as with a flood, to gather out mine elect from the four quarters of the earth, unto a place which I shall prepare, an Holy City, that my people may gird up their loins, and be

looking forth for the time of my coming; for there shall be my tabernacle, and it shall be called Zion, a New Jerusalem" (Moses 7:62).

Consider the events of our dispensation as Enoch describes them.
First, we are told that righteousness will be sent down out of heaven.
That would embrace all the revelations and angelic ministrants that
have been associated with the restoration of the gospel to the Prophet
Joseph Smith. Christ himself, earlier in the same revelation, bears
the title "the Righteous" (see Moses 7:45, 47), suggesting to me that
this outpouring from the heavens begins with his appearance in the
Sacred Grove. Then comes the announcement that truth will be
brought forth out of the earth. Thus the testimony of heaven and
earth combine to testify of Christ and the saving truths of his gospel.
The description that follows in Enoch's vision tells us that the truth
from the earth will testify of the Only Begotten and his resurrection
from the dead and the resurrection of all mankind. No book on earth
fits that description as dramatically or perfectly as the Book of
Mormon.

As one of the early Brethren observed of similar prophecies in
the Bible, if this is not a description of the Book of Mormon, then
we wait for another book to come forth in the same manner which
contains the same story and teaches the same truths. Then we are
told, as Enoch's vision continues, that the truths that have been
restored from the heavens and those that have come forth from the
earth will unite to sweep the earth as with a flood to gather out the
Lord's elect. It would take some effort to miss the message that the
revelations of the Restoration in company with the Book of Mormon
constitute the message that is to gather Israel. What we have *not* read
here is that strong arguments about the true meaning of the Bible
will convert and gather Israel. The testimony that will revolutionize
the religious world is to come anew from the heavens and from the
earth. It will bear the label "modern revelation" and come forth in a
miraculous manner. Thereafter a holy city will be established and a

people prepared for the return of Christ. In the midst of that city will be the Lord's tabernacle (meaning temple), and the city shall be called Zion or the New Jerusalem.

WE CANNOT ISOLATE THE BOOK OF MORMON

One most important truth to be learned from Enoch's vision is that it was not intended that the Book of Mormon carry the full burden of gathering Israel. Although it contains the doctrines of salvation in simplicity and purity and was ordained in the councils of heaven to actuate the gathering of Israel, and although no other scriptural text can match its witness of Christ and the resurrection, it was not intended that the Book of Mormon stand alone in the fulfillment of its divinely decreed destiny. As Enoch notes, the revelations of heaven in union with the truth from the earth were to visit every clime and sweep every country. We must do more than just flood the earth with copies of the Book of Mormon. Our message is not the Book of Mormon. It is the restored gospel, of which the Book of Mormon is the best evidence. To be meaningful, the Book of Mormon must be distributed in the context of the Restoration. It does not and cannot stand independent of the authority restored by John the Baptist to baptize for the remission of sins or the authority restored by Peter, James, and John by which the gift of the Holy Ghost is bestowed. The constitution of the Church must always be the voice of living prophets and the keys and authority they possess. This authority alone can authorize the performance of the ordinances of salvation.

It is not the idea that we gather the Lord's elect to a book, and for that matter, it is not the idea that we gather them to a particular land, either. Salvation is not found by professing faith in a book or by inhabiting a particular plot of ground. We gather Israel to the truths and ordinances of salvation. We gather them to the waters of baptism and the ordinances of the house of the Lord. In the performance of those sacred ordinances, the promises made to the fathers become a reality for their posterity. Lands of inheritance are simply a tangible token of promises made to those who keep their covenants with exactness and honor. Thus the promise, as we have already noted, is "in bringing about his covenants and his gospel unto those who are of the house of Israel" (1 Nephi 22:11).

WE STAND INDEPENDENT

The gospel has been restored "that all that will hear may hear" the message of salvation (D&C 1:11). All are to receive that message, our revelations declare, "by the mouths of" those whom the Lord sends (D&C 1:4). Though the spreading of the gospel will be aided by mass communication media, such media will never replace personal contact between members and investigators. Reading the Book of Mormon will not remit sins, nor can radios baptize or televisions convey the gift of the Holy Ghost. The promise that the arm of the Lord will be revealed will find its primary fulfillment through those who go forth endowed with power from on high to teach his gospel and bear testimony of him. "I call upon the weak things of the world," the Lord said, "those who are unlearned and despised, to thrash the nations by the power of my Spirit; and their arm shall be my arm, and I will be their shield and their buckler; and I will gird up their loins, and they shall fight manfully for me; and their enemies shall be under their feet; and I will let fall the sword in their behalf, and by the fire of mine indignation will I preserve them" (D&C 35:13–14).

There is no reservation in heaven about what can be accomplished by those whom the Lord chooses to send to declare his message. Many in the world falsely suppose that when God has spoken through his prophets, the process involves what they have chosen to call divine dictation. The idea is that for the mind and will of God to be conveyed in such a manner that it is not contaminated in any way by the weakness of the flesh, all bodily functions of the Lord's spokesman are temporarily suspended when the Lord speaks through him. Thus the role of the prophet becomes that of a dummy in the lap of the divine ventriloquist. The prophet is simply the voice through whom the Lord speaks and has no more effect on the message than a radio does on the words of the one speaking through it.

Nothing could be further from the truth. Explaining the process by which revelation comes, the Lord told Oliver Cowdery that He would speak to him in his mind and in his heart (see D&C 8:2). That is to say, there are no mindless or heartless revelations. God gave us our minds to use, and the primary way in which they ought to be used is to obtain his mind and will. In like manner, he gave us our hearts, our emotions and feelings, and he expects these too to be used in obtaining his will. The more perfectly our minds and hearts are tuned to the Spirit of the Lord, the more perfect will be our communication with him. We do not suspend our God-given endowments to communicate with God; rather, we expand their capacity. That is done by the aid of the Spirit, and the Spirit in turn is aided by the preparations we have made in complying with and studying the laws and ordinances of the gospel. As puny preparation will precede puny revelations, so those who prepare themselves to be a source of light to others will find that light growing brighter and brighter until the perfect day (see D&C 50:24). Where there is no depth of soil, there can be no depth of root (see Matthew 13:18–23).

The salient point is that the way we present our message has much to do with the kind of people who accept it and the depth of commitment they have in doing so. There is a difference between the commitment of individuals who join the Church only because they were impressed with a gifted entertainer or talented athlete and that of individuals who join the Church because they have feasted on the Book of Mormon and proved it true in their own sacred grove. Likewise, there is a difference between the commitment of someone who has joined the Church because we have convinced them that we share common ground with the rest of the Christian world but have given it a new and exciting twist and that of someone who understands that there has been a new dispensation of the gospel whereby we stand entirely independent of the rest of the religious world. The more faithful we are to the message the Lord has given us, the more completely we teach the message of the Restoration, the deeper and richer the soil will be in which we plant the seeds of everlasting life, and the better the fruits it will produce in the realms of faith and loyalty to the gospel cause. Our spiritual stability is measured by our loyalty to the teachings of the Prophet Joseph Smith.

The stake in which my family lives recently participated in a regional conference. A flyer dropped off at our home encouraging our attendance at this meeting made a special point to tell us that a member of the Quorum of the Twelve and two other General Authorities would be in attendance. We, of course, were excited about the prospects of a spiritual feast and made it a point to go early in the hopes of getting a good seat. On that matter we were a little disappointed because so many of our neighbors had the same idea. Conversely, however, a goodly number chose not to come. They saw it as a chance to get a break in their regular Sunday responsibilities and not be missed. I would not be surprised to discover that among those who chose not to attend the regional meeting were some who spent part of that time in prayer and scripture study. One way to test the appropriateness of such an action is to ask, What would happen if everyone did the same thing? In this instance, the answer would be that contact with the living oracles would be lost and our religion, like that of traditional Christianity, would be limited to what had been given in times past. Similarly, if such a course became the established pattern among those who stayed home, their reverence for the Lord's servants would shift from living oracles to dead ones. Scriptural history evidences that such a course always leads to disastrous results. But what of their prayers? Would they be answered? The testimony of scripture unites very eloquently to declare that our refusal to listen when the Lord sends his messengers to us will bring a very abrupt halt to any communication we might hope to obtain from him.

Does this principle apply any differently in our efforts to share the restored gospel with others? That is, if we insist in proving the tenets of our faith from Bible texts rather than from the revelations of the Restoration or the statements of our living oracles, are we not approaching the gospel in the same spirit as those who chose to stay home with their scriptures over hearing the words of those we sustain as prophets, seers, and revelators? And, if that is the example we set in teaching the gospel to investigators, do we have any right to act surprised when we discover their roots are not sunk as deeply in the soil of faith as they need to be to survive the storms that inevitably descend upon them?

The truths of salvation can be found only in the dispensation of which we are a part. For those of our day, those truths are not to be found in Enoch's city or Noah's ark, nor can they be found in a return to Sinai or the attempt to reconstruct the message of Christ from the New Testament. After writing his Gospel, John said, "And there are also many other things which Jesus did, the which, if they should be written every one, I suppose that even the world itself could not contain the books that should be written" (John 21:25). From the writings of Luke we learn that the teachings and experiences that converted the Twelve are not recorded within the pages of the New Testament but were associated with the forty-day ministry that began after the Gospel writers concluded their story (see Acts 1:1–4). In his epistles, Paul did not quote from the Gospel writers, suggesting that their records were not extant during the time he wrote, or, at least, that he had no knowledge of them. Paul declared the source of his gospel to be revelation (see Galatians 1:6–12).

Each gospel dispensation is rooted in a revelation of its own, a revelation that allows it to stand independent with its own oracle at the head. The great test of each dispensation is in looking past the frailties of its oracle to accept the blessings of the truths of salvation at his hand.

NOTES

1. *Utah Genealogical and Historical Magazine* 23 (October 1932): 175.

2. See Joseph Smith, *Teachings of the Prophet Joseph Smith*, sel. Joseph Fielding Smith (Salt Lake City: Deseret Book, 1974), p. 121.

Chapter Seven

TEACHING PURE DOCTRINE

Again I say, hearken ye elders of my church, whom I have appointed:
Ye are not sent forth to be taught, but to teach the children of men the
things which I have put into your hands by the power of my Spirit;
*   And ye are to be taught from on high. Sanctify yourselves and ye shall*
be endowed with power, that ye may give even as I have spoken.
         —Doctrine and Covenants 43:15–16

AS HE WAITED FOR HIS flight to be announced, my father buried himself in a book by a renowned New Testament scholar. He was delighted to discover material by a sectarian scholar that constituted a marvelous defense of Mormonism. As he boarded the flight he met Marion G. Romney, then a member of the First Presidency. He said, "President Romney, I have got to read this to you. This is good," and proceeded to share his newfound treasure. When he was finished, President Romney said, "Bruce, I have to tell you a story. A few years ago I found something that I thought was remarkable written by one of the world's great scholars. I read it to J. Reuben Clark, and he said, 'Look, when you read things like that, and you find that the world doesn't agree with us, so what? And when you read something like that and you find they are right on the mark and they agree with us, so what?'"

My father thought that a good lesson. The world is not the source of the doctrines we teach nor is it the source from which we seek confirmation for our doctrines. We simply do not bear testimony on the basis of the wisdom of the world. Doctrine and testimony must come from a pure source. To get that idea across to his children, Dad used a little cowboy wisdom. "Don't drink below the horses," he said. "All true religion is revealed religion." Which is simply to say, we must drink at the fountainhead.

In so saying I am not picking a fight with good scholarship. My father read widely. He had a fine library of well-read books. He read the best of Latter-day Saint writers and the best of secular scholars. His standard of measure, however, was always the revealed gospel.

DOCTRINES OF SALVATION

A doctrine is something learned, because, as the word *doctrine* implies, it is something taught. The source of all good doctrine must be God himself. If a doctrine cannot clearly demonstrate its divine origin, it cannot claim place in the family of saving principles. Members of the Church share a loyalty to and a faith in certain principles we accept as doctrines of salvation. By revelation the Lord said, "For thus shall my church be called in the last days, even The Church of Jesus Christ of Latter-day Saints" (D&C 115:4). *The* in the name of the Church carries a meaning quite different from *a*

Church of Jesus Christ. To say it is *the* Church is to say, as the Lord did in the first section of the Doctrine and Covenants, that it is the "only true and living church upon the face of the whole earth" (D&C 1:30). We hold that declaration to be a doctrine of salvation. Salvation cannot be found in any other organization, ordinances, priesthood, or doctrines. Needless to say, that announcement has given offense to many. Doctrines created in heaven never seem to find a comfortable resting place in theologies crafted by the wisdom of men.

No saving doctrine can stand independent of faith in Christ and the necessary discipline associated with membership in his church. Saving doctrines do not grow wild. Salvation is not found in everyone doing his own thing. Those who falsely suppose that they can negotiate their own salvation often choose to be offended by such declarations. If, as Latter-day Saints hold, there is only one true church, then all others are false and thus the doctrines of salvation are not found in them. Such a position, we are frequently assured, is both judgmental and unchristian. The irony of such an accusation should not go unnoticed. To be Christian, in any meaningful sense of the word, is to believe that the hope of salvation is in Christ. It is to embrace the dogma that mankind is in a fallen state from which Christ alone can redeem them. Thus, all who make a serious profession to being Christians must draw the same narrow and judgmental line relative to Christ that Latter-day Saints draw relative to his Church and its doctrines. The real issue is not the necessity of drawing such a line but rather where it should be drawn and who has the authority to draw it.

DOCTRINAL DECOYS

The essence of our faith centers on preserving the purity of our doctrine. No principle of salvation can ever be a matter of private interpretation or of speculation. Faith cannot be exercised in principles that are not true. As we must not be seduced by false doctrines, so we must not be distracted by doctrinal decoys. Let me suggest a few of the common forms such decoys take.

Irrelevant Testimony

When I was a young seminary student, our teacher gave a lesson for which he placed pictures of a dozen world-renowned scientists in the front of the room. Then he read a quotation from each of the men represented, in which they indicated a belief in God. The idea was that we shared a faith in common with these great scientists and thus our faith was justified. In truth that is not the case. What they were calling God, we call nature. The statements he read merely illustrated that these men acknowledge that there is order in the laws of nature and that those laws govern our universe. The faith, however, that God is a personal being, that he is the father of our spirits, that he was literally the father of Jesus of Nazareth, that Jesus worked out an atoning sacrifice that assures that we will all be resurrected and if we choose to live worthy may return to the presence of God, is quite another matter. If any of those men embraced that faith, which is peculiar to Latter-day Saints, then why hadn't they numbered themselves among us? And if they had, then their testimony of God, of necessity, would have rested on spiritual, not scientific, principles. I assume they were all wise and good men, but their affirmation of God's existence rested on their wisdom, not on the revelations of heaven.

A Bible scholar of considerable reputation recently told a group of divinity students at an Ivy League school that Joseph Smith was a prophet just as Moses was a prophet. The statement loses much of its luster, however, with the discovery of what this man really thinks of Moses. Academic acknowledgments and spiritual commitment are not the same thing. Had he lived in the days of Moses, this man would not have followed him any more than he would now seek admission into the Church by confession of his sins and baptism at the hands of our young missionaries.

Proof Texts

Those advocating questionable doctrines or practices will virtually always seek to give them credibility through the use of proof texts from scripture. Two characteristics are common to such efforts. First, the texts will be obscure, in sharp contrast to the principles of salvation that are taught repeatedly throughout the scriptures. Second, they will be strained; the burden they are being forced to bear will not be natural to them. That is to say, they will not be justified by the context from which they are taken.

Let me cite two illustrations. Sectarian creeds declare God to be "without body, parts, or passions." The text that bears the weight of that declaration is John 4:24, which states, "God is a spirit." The difficulty here is at least twofold. First, an assertion of such importance, one that is announcing the very nature of God, ought not rest on a single scriptural text. The burden is simply too great for a four-word sentence to carry. That has to be particularly true when the sentence is being given an interpretation that puts it at odds with hosts of other scriptural texts that describe the bodily appearance of God to prophets and others. Second, and paradoxically, this is one of the key texts used in the early Christian era to argue precisely the opposite point. If God was a spirit, it was argued, he must have both bodily form and material substance from which his spirit was made, so he obviously could not be without body and parts. That was the notion fought against by those advocating the doctrine embraced in Christian creeds that God was without body and parts. John 4:24 was one of the passages most often quoted against those efforts. What we have here, then, is the typical obscure text being called upon to bear a burden that is out of harmony with the preponderance of

Bible texts and that is out of harmony with the context in which it was originally understood.[1]

As a second illustration, let's take the overworked statement of Christ to Simon Peter: "Thou art Peter, and upon this rock I will build my church. . . . And I will give unto thee the keys of the kingdom of heaven" (Matthew 16:18–19). From this text it is argued that Peter was to be the rock upon which the Church was to rest and that he was to hold the keys of the same. One great difficulty here is that when Christ did in fact give the keys, he gave them to all of the Twelve rather than to Peter alone (Matthew 18:18–20; John 20:19–23). As to the immediate context, the subject being discussed is how Peter knows that Jesus is the Christ. He is being commended for having obtained that knowledge by the spirit of revelation. Having commended Peter for obtaining his understanding by the Spirit of revelation, Christ says, "Upon this rock [i.e., the rock of revelation] I will build my church." Again the greater issue becomes, can a single phrase be called upon to bear the doctrinal burden placed upon it? Or ought such matters, like all other principles of salvation, be taught both plainly and repetitiously? Surely it must stretch the credulity of honest truth-seekers to suppose that a man rather than God is the foundation of a heaven-sent kingdom.

The Wisdom of Men

The purity of the gospel is lost when scripture is mingled with the philosophies of men. The center of gravity for the Christian world was shifted in the time between the death of the apostles and the Council of Nicaea in A.D. 325. A church that had been founded on the principle of revelation was now to be founded on philosophical speculation. A form of godliness was preserved, but the power was lost, and the world entered into a period known to us as the Dark Ages. The loss to mankind has been immeasurable, and even though the gospel has now been restored, it will be generations before its influence will set at naught the influence of those dark days. Isaiah, describing these events, said people would honor the Lord with their mouths but their hearts would be far from him because their reverence for him had been taught them "by the precept of men." For that reason, he said, the Lord would "work a marvellous work and a wonder" among them, one which would cause "the wisdom of their wise men" to perish, and "the understanding of their prudent men" to be hid (Isaiah 29:13–14).

Nephi, in a prophetic description of the churches of the last days, said that all had gone astray, "save it be a few," whom he depicted as the "humble followers of Christ." Nevertheless, he said, even they had been led astray in many instances because they had been "taught by the precepts of men" (2 Nephi 28:14). We have no shortage of scriptural warnings against putting our trust in the arm of flesh, for, as Nephi said, "cursed is he that putteth his trust in the arm of flesh" (2 Nephi 4:34).

One seductive danger vying for the attentions of Latter-day Saints is the temptation to substitute various "evidences" for faith. I am not suggesting that ours should be an unreasoned faith, that it cannot bear rigorous examination, or that we are expected to check our minds at the door when we go into church. I am suggesting that our doctrinal understanding must be grounded in faith and that no amount of man-made wisdom can substitute for it. Indeed, our earthly probation was intended as a test of faith, not a test of intellect. That test must of necessity include things that defy the intellect. "We speak," Paul said, "not in the words which man's wisdom teacheth, but which the Holy Ghost teacheth; comparing spiritual things with spiritual." And we do so, knowing that "the natural man receiveth not the things of the Spirit of God: for they are foolishness unto him: neither can he know them, because they are spiritually discerned" (1 Corinthians 2:13–14).

Let me suggest an illustration. The Lord invited us to discover the truthfulness of the Book of Mormon by the power of the Holy Ghost (see Moroni 10:3–5). Significantly, Mormon, the book's editor, warned that it was given in the form it was so that it would constitute a test of faith. He said: "And when they [those of our day] shall have received this [the Book of Mormon], which is expedient that they should have first [before we get the complete account of the Savior's teachings to the Nephites and the sealed portion of the plates], to try their faith, and if it shall so be that they shall believe these things then shall the greater things be made manifest unto them. And if it so be that they will not believe these things, then shall the greater things be withheld from them, unto their condemnation. Behold, I was about to write them, all which were engraven upon the plates of Nephi, but the Lord forbade it, saying: I will try the faith of my people" (3 Nephi 26:9–11).

Now, given that it is the Lord's purpose that our testimony of the Book of Mormon rest on faith, what is our purpose in so zealously seeking evidences of all sorts to respond to whatever issues in the book require faith to accept? If such evidence supplants the necessity of faith, are we not at odds with the Lord's purposes? I do not desire to be misunderstood here. We are obligated to bring the best of our scholarship to bear on the study of the Book of Mormon and all other scriptural records. We do not have the right to do less, but we cannot substitute the evidences of men for the witnesses of the Spirit. Scholarly decoys are the danger here. Some seem to be more interested in proving the Book of Mormon true than in discovering what it actually teaches. The irony is that the only meaningful evidence that the book is true is its doctrines. Faith is available to all on equal grounds, as are answers to prayers—scholarly understanding is not. When those who do not have the necessary academic skills are induced to build the house of their understanding of blocks supplied by scholars, they become beholden to the scholars. They find themselves out of context. The scholar then stands between them and God. That is precisely what happened in the Great Apostasy and brought the meridian dispensation to an end. Scholars replaced prophets, and the gospel was declared a mystery that could be understood only by those who had been schooled and trained for the ministry. Thus the trained minister was placed between the believer and God.

Substituting Ethics for Doctrine

"We are to teach the principles of the gospel. We are to teach the doctrines of salvation," stated Elder Bruce R. McConkie. "We have some passing interest in ethical principles but not a great deal as far as emphasis in teaching is concerned. If we teach the doctrines of salvation, the ethical concepts automatically follow. We do not need to spend long periods of time or make elaborate presentations in teaching honesty or integrity or unselfishness or some other ethical principle. Any Presbyterian can do that. Any Methodist can do that. But if we teach the doctrines of salvation, which are basic and fundamental, the ethical concepts automatically follow. It is the testimony and knowledge of the truth that causes people to reach high ethical standards in any event. And so our revelation says: 'And I give unto you a commandment [again we are using mandatory language; the Lord is talking] that you shall teach one another the doctrine of the kingdom'" [D&C 88:77].[2]

President J. Reuben Clark Jr. observed: "One living, burning, honest testimony of a righteous God-fearing man that Jesus is the Christ and that Joseph was God's prophet, is worth a thousand books and lectures aimed at debasing the Gospel to a system of ethics or seeking to rationalize infinity."[3]

PURE DOCTRINE MUST COME FROM A PURE SOURCE

We have in the missionary experiences of the Apostle Paul a marvelous story illustrating that if a testimony of truth comes from the wrong source it is not acceptable to God. On the Sabbath day it was the practice of the Saints in Philippi to meet outside the city wall at a place along the river that ran nearby. In one such meeting they were joined by a slave girl who was possessed by "a spirit of divination," which enabled her to tell fortunes and thus make considerable money for her masters. "The same followed Paul and us [Luke is telling the story], and cried, saying, These men are the servants of the most high God, which shew unto us the way of salvation" (Acts 16:17). This sequence repeated itself for many days.

Here was a young woman who was possessed with the spirit of the devil, yet her testimony was true. She repeatedly testified that Paul and Luke were servants of the most high God and that by listening to them the people could learn the principles of salvation. Why would one possessed with the spirit of the adversary bear such a testimony? In considering these verses the question is frequently asked, Can the devil teach truth? The answer, as the story illustrates, is yes, he can and will teach truth when it suits his purpose. What he cannot do is teach it by the Spirit of truth. Consider his purpose in this instance. Jewish law abhorred magical rites and dealings with familiar spirits. Thus, for Paul and his companions to leave the young damsel's testimony unchallenged would have closed the door to proselyting in the Jewish community. By contrast, fortune-telling was popular among the Gentiles. Acceptance of the damsel's testimony would have had the effect in the Gentile community of saying, "Look, the Christian message is not really any different from what we have. When you get down to it, all religion is really the same." As to those of the household of faith, to accept such a testimony would grant this soothsayer credence among their number and thus give the voice of the adversary place among the Saints. Because the experience was new to Paul and his companions, they were not immediately certain how they should respond, but eventually they came to realize what action must be taken, and thus Paul commanded the evil spirit to depart (see Acts 16:18).

The issue here is not one of truth, meaning correctness. What the damsel testified to was true: Paul and his companions were authorized servants of the God of heaven. They represented the source of saving truths to that people. At issue was the source of the damsel's truth. It did not come from God, it did not and could not bear his Spirit, nor could it bear the fruits of that Spirit. Pure doctrine can be taught only from a pure source and for pure reasons. Paul's experience reminds us that when those with "unclean spirits" fell before Christ and cried aloud saying, "Thou art the Son of God," he "straitly charged them that they should not make him known" (Mark 3:11–12). Similarly, when the man in the synagogue who was possessed with an unclean spirit testified that Jesus was the "holy One of God," the Savior rebuked him and cast the evil spirit out of him (Mark 1:23–25).

Nowhere is this doctrine taught with greater plainness than in Doctrine and Covenants 50. In a setting where various spirits had manifested themselves in the youthful church in false visions, phony revelations, and other strange phenomena, the Lord established a standard for pure doctrine. He did so in a series of rhetorical questions. First, he asked, "Unto what were ye ordained?" To which his own answer is: "To preach my gospel [and none other] by the Spirit," meaning "the Comforter," which has been "sent forth to teach the truth." Then, by way of commentary, the Lord said, "He that is ordained of me and sent forth to preach the word of truth by the Comforter, in the Spirit of truth, doth he preach it by the Spirit of truth or some other way?" Clearly, the Lord is telling us that the gospel can be taught in ways other than by his Spirit. Thus he said, "If it be by some other way it is not of God" (D&C 50:13–18).

The message is simple enough: both the gospel and the spirit by which it is taught must come from the same source. Anything else would be an impure doctrine. It is the waters of everlasting life of which we speak. No one wants to drink water that is impure, and no one wants to drink pure water that has been placed in an impure container.

Obviously, it is important that the doctrinal waters we drink are pure. That requires that our experiences with the Spirit be immediate and personal. Generally we do that by obtaining the confirmation of the Spirit of that which the scriptures and the Lord's anointed are teaching. When the principles of salvation are at stake, we cannot afford to trust other sources. A colleague of mine bought bottled water in Egypt at discount prices from little boys on the street only to find that they had been doing their own bottling. He, as would be expected, got sick. This is not to say that we cannot obtain doctrinal insights from other sources. Of course we can. The world and everything in it is our textbook for understanding and teaching the gospel. We do not, however, turn to the world to obtain the gospel or look to it as the source of our testimony; but, having received the gospel through the channels the Lord has ordained, we can use art, music, science, literature, or whatever resources we have at our command to illustrate its principles.

Those bearing the gospel message have been told, "Ye are not sent forth to be taught, but to teach the children of men the things which I have put into your hands by the power of my Spirit; and ye are to be taught from on high. Sanctify yourselves and ye shall be endowed with power, that ye may give even as I have spoken" (D&C 43:15–16). Ours is a limited commission; we are to teach only those things that the Lord has given us to teach. There are many perceptive and wise things we can learn from the world. Certainly we should know and share the same, but not in the name of the Lord and not in lieu of the message he has given us to bear.

Christ in dialogue with his disciples asked, "Whom do men say that I the Son of man am?" Simon Peter responded, "Thou art the

Christ, the Son of the living God." Jesus then said, "Blessed art thou, Simon Bar-jona: for flesh and blood hath not revealed it unto thee, but my Father which is in heaven" (Matthew 16:13, 16–17). Thus Peter is commended not simply for knowing the truth of Christ's divine origin but for knowing it from the right source. He had not learned it from "flesh and blood," meaning mortal man or other earthbound sources, but rather by the Spirit of revelation, which is the foundation upon which all true religion must rest.

ALL TRUE DOCTRINE MUST COME FROM THE FATHER

All true doctrine, that is, all truths that have the power of salvation in them, originate with and are sent forth by the Father. He is the author of the gospel and creator of the plan of salvation. He ordained the laws whereby all his spirit children, Christ included, might advance and progress and become like him. It is his gospel. It is his plan of salvation that called for the creation and peopling of the earth, for the fall of Adam and the resultant probationary estate of man, for the atonement of the Lord Jesus Christ, for the immortality and eternal life of man, and for all the glories and wonders of eternity.

Even Jesus did not purport to originate doctrine. Malachi referred to him as the "messenger of the covenant" (Malachi 3:1), and modern revelation calls him "the messenger of salvation" (D&C 93:8). Of his New Testament teachings Christ said, "My doctrine is not mine, but his that sent me" (John 7:16). Among the Nephites the resurrected Christ said, "This is my doctrine, and it is the doctrine which the Father hath given unto me" (3 Nephi 11:32) and also, "I came into the world to do the will of my Father, because my Father sent me" (3 Nephi 27:13). A true prophet has no doctrine of his own. Like Christ, he is a messenger of the covenant. "If any man will do his [meaning the Father's] will, he shall know of the doctrine, whether it be of God, or whether I speak of myself," the Savior said (John 7:16–17). Nor is it any different with the word declared by any of the prophets who speak in the name of the Lord. All those who conform to the will of the Lord, walking in obedience to his commandments, shall know whether the doctrine came from God or was devised by the minds of men.

True doctrine will always trace itself to the Father. We would hardly expect the Savior to come on the scene saying, "My Father said such and such, but in my judgment it ought to be otherwise." Were that his example, it would give us all license to remake the gospel to suit our own purposes. For the same reason the prophets and apostles of the Lord don't come to us and say, "Well, the Lord said this, but I think it ought to be something else." Again, that would destroy the gospel. Their message must be one with that of the Father and the Son. And so it is with each of us. There never was a soul in earth's history who had the right to add to or take from the gospel. Plenty of people assume the prerogative to modify what the Lord or his prophets have said. For them, salvation is found in everyone's doing his own thing. A recent advertising campaign for a local church illustrates. It begins, "You don't have to see God as straight, white, and a man." It then invites those with deviant lifestyles to join in their worship service, announcing that their attitude "goes way beyond tolerance" to "encourage diversity." We are left to wonder how the statement of the Lord that "if ye are not one ye are not mine" (D&C 38:27) fits in with all of that.

All prophets preach the same doctrine. That is not to say that they all share the same depth of understanding. Some, a Joseph Smith for instance, have a much greater endowment in the realm of spiritual understanding than do others. And the difference between what is taught by divinely commissioned messengers in various ages is dictated in large measure by the spiritual maturity of those to whom they have been sent. "It is given unto many to know the mysteries of God," Alma said, "nevertheless they are laid under strict command that they shall not impart only according to the portion of his word which he doth grant unto the children of men, according to the heed and diligence which they give unto him" (Alma 12:9). Men are given only such portion of the mind and will and word of the Lord as their spiritual stature entitles them to receive.

The word of the Lord is always the same; God does not change. Gospel truths do not adjust themselves to the winds of fashion; gospel ordinances always serve the same purposes; and the same gospel rewards always come by obedience to the same laws. Adam, Enoch, Noah, Abraham, Moses, and all the prophets and Saints of all ages had faith in the same God, believed the same doctrines, lived the same laws, and have gone on to the same eternal rewards. In each instance the people of that day were expected to learn the principles of the gospel from the prophet appointed to preside over them and to receive the ordinances of salvation under his hand. Individuals must accept the message of salvation from the prophets sent them. They cannot gaze fondly back to former days and expect to gain the blessings of heaven. One reason is that the message of salvation requires the performance of ordinances. Thus, those who embrace it must do so at the hands of a living administrator. A dead prophet, no matter how great he was, cannot baptize anyone. A second reason is that it brings us back to the necessity of faith. Little faith is needed to believe in dead prophets, who inevitably enjoy the acclaim of the world. Living prophets are another matter. To follow a living prophet always requires both faith and courage. It always places one at odds with the world. That is the reason that though we quote, use, expound, teach from, and glory in the Bible, we understand it is not the source of doctrine nor the hope of salvation to those of our dispensation. No people believe the Bible more devoutly than the Latter-day Saints. We cannot speak too highly of it, yet it is not a source of priesthood nor does it stand at the head of the Church. When we go

forth to teach the doctrines of salvation, our divine commission—
the commandment given us—is to teach the revelations and commandments that have come to and through Joseph Smith. "By them,"
meaning the revelations of our dispensation, "shall the world be
judged," the Lord said, "even as many as shall hereafter come to a
knowledge of this work. And those who receive it [the Book of
Mormon] in faith, and work righteousness, shall receive a crown of
eternal life; but those who harden their hearts in unbelief, and reject
it, it shall turn to their own condemnation" (D&C 20:13–15).

THE CHANNEL ORDAINED FOR OUR DAY

Many in the world today profess to accept Jesus or to embrace
the Christian faith. For that faith to be pure, the source of that faith
must also be pure. In his visit to the Nephites, Christ reviewed the
prophetic promises relative to the latter-day gathering of Israel. He
told them that Israel would be gathered when the Book of Mormon
came forth and that the rightful heirs of those promises would be
those who accepted the testimony of that scriptural record.
"Therefore it shall come to pass that whosoever will not believe in
my words, who am Jesus Christ, which the Father shall cause him
[Joseph Smith] to bring forth unto the Gentiles, and shall give unto
him power that he shall bring them forth unto the Gentiles, (it shall
be done even as Moses said) they shall be cut off from among my
people who are of the covenant" (3 Nephi 21:11). That is to say,
Joseph Smith and the Book of Mormon constitute the channel, or
source, of the testimony of Christ for our dispensation. No other
source fills the prophecy, and no other source has the power of salvation in it. Those who profess Christ while rejecting the Book of
Mormon are to be "cut off" from the blessings of the covenant and
will be left, in the language of Malachi, which the Savior also quoted
to the Nephites, with "neither root nor branch" (3 Nephi 25:1).

To be left with "neither root nor branch," meaning ancestry or posterity, is to be left without a place in an eternal family unit on the Day of Judgment. It is to be left without progenitors or posterity, whereas the covenant made with Abraham centered on the continuation of the family unit. The promise of those blessings is found only in the temple and comes only at the hands of those authorized to perform such ordinances. To reject the testimony of Christ as it comes to us through Joseph Smith and the Book of Mormon is to reject those blessings.

By revelation we have been told that the higher priesthood is to "administer the gospel," meaning that it is the source through which it is to come both to us and to all nations of the earth (see D&C 84:19). Joseph Smith said, "The Melchizedek Priesthood . . . is the channel through which all knowledge, doctrine, the plan of salvation and every important matter is revealed from heaven."[4] Thus every doctrine we espouse must, if it be a pure doctrine, trace itself to that priesthood restored to Joseph Smith and Oliver Cowdery by Peter, James, and John. It must represent the opening of the heavens, the reality of living prophets in our day, and a people who stand independent of the world and of their religious traditions. Few waters have been as muddied as those of religious tradition. We must, if our doctrine is to be pure, drink at the fountainhead. That is tantamount to saying that any doctrine that does not bear the label "revelation" is not our doctrine and is unworthy of our faith. We have not built out of the theological rubble of the past. Every priesthood, key, power, authority, or doctrine necessary for the salvation of men must be rooted in this the dispensation of the fulness of times.

Brigham Young calls our attention to another principle relative to things coming through the proper channels. He said, "If the Lord Almighty should reveal to a High Priest, or to any other than the head, things that are true, or that have been and will be, and show to him the destiny of this people twenty-five years from now, or a new doctrine that will in five, ten, or twenty years hence become the doctrine of this Church and Kingdom, but which has not yet been revealed to this people, and reveal it to him by the same Spirit, the same messenger, the same voice, the same power that gave revelations to Joseph when he was living, it would be a blessing to that High Priest, or individual; but he must rarely divulge it to a second person on the face of the earth, until God reveals it through the proper source to become the property of the people at large. Therefore when you hear Elders say that God does not reveal through the President of the Church that which they know, and tell wonderful things, you may generally set it down as God's truth that the revelation they have had is from the Devil, and not from God. If they had received from the proper source, the same power that revealed it to them would have shown them that they must keep the things revealed in their own bosoms, and they seldom would have a desire to disclose them to the second person."[5]

THE CONSTITUTION OF THE CHURCH

Living prophets are the constitution of the Church. Some have erroneously supposed that the New Testament was the guiding document of the meridian Church. This could not have been the case. None of its books was written in the lifetime of Christ. Thessalonians, written in A.D. 52, is believed to be the first of the New Testament books to have been penned. The next half century witnessed the writing of the others, and then more than three hundred years passed before these books were bound together in one cover. Thus the Apostasy was complete before the New Testament as we know it existed.

Paul testified that apostles and prophets were the foundation of the meridian Church (Ephesians 2:20). When he said, "God hath set some in the church, first apostles, secondarily prophets, thirdly teachers"

(1 Corinthians 12:28), he was not thinking of those who had passed beyond the veil. The Old Testament, for all of its greatness and inspiration, could not direct a New Testament church. The very idea of a "new testament," or more properly a "new covenant," assured the reality of an independent dispensation—a day of revelation. As to our own day, if we are to lay claim to a "true and living church," then it must have a true and living constitution, that is, living prophets and apostles.

Joseph Smith gave a committee headed by John Taylor the assignment to write a constitution for the kingdom of God. Their efforts were fruitless. Unable to lay claim to inspiration, they reported back to the Prophet. He matter-of-factly acknowledged their failure, stating that "they could not draft a constitution worthy of guiding the kingdom of God" and that he had gone before the Lord seeking that such a constitution be granted by revelation. In response to his entreaties, the Lord said, "Ye are my constitution and I am your God and ye are my spokesman, therefore from henceforth keep my commandments."[6]

Years later when John Taylor was president of the Church, a revelation given to the Church stated: "Ye have not chosen me, but I have chosen you. I called you by my servant Joseph, and by my servant Brigham, and by my servant John. You did not teach and instruct me; but I have taught and instructed you and organized you according to my eternal laws. Ye are my Constitution, and I am your God; and I will be acknowledged; and my will and my word and my law shall bear rule in my Kingdom, saith the Lord. If it does not, then it is not my Kingdom, and then are ye not my spokesmen; saith the Lord. For if it is by the wisdom of man, by the intelligence of man, and under the direction of man, then it is a Kingdom of man and not of me, and I acknowledge it not, saith the Lord God. Have I not instructed you in all that you know, and is not this Kingdom organized and directed by revelation from me? Is it not called the Kingdom of God? If, therefore, it is not my Kingdom, why do you make use of my name and invoke my authority and my aid? Is this Kingdom not called, the kingdom of God and his laws, with the keys and power thereof, and judgment in the hands of his servants. Amen Christ."[7]

WHERE TO EXPECT FALSE DOCTRINE

"Among the Latter-day Saints, the preaching of false doctrines disguised as truths of the gospel, may be expected from people of two classes, and practically from these only," observed President Joseph F. Smith. "They are," he said:

"First—The hopelessly ignorant, whose lack of intelligence is due to their indolence and sloth, who make but feeble effort, if indeed any at all, to better themselves by reading and study; those who are afflicted with a dread disease that may develop into an incurable malady—laziness.

"Second—The proud and self-vaunting ones, who read by the lamp of their own conceit; who interpret by rules of their own contriving; who have become a law unto themselves, and so pose as the sole judges of their own doings. More dangerously ignorant than the first.

"Beware of the lazy and the proud; their infection in each case is contagious; better for them and for all when they are compelled to display the yellow flag of warning, that the clean and uninfected may be protected."[8]

WHY SOME ARE UNCOMFORTABLE WITH DOCTRINES

To those outside the faith, or those within the Church who are not fully converted, doctrines are often viewed as being arbitrary, authoritarian, and intolerant. Such people consistently seek to dissociate God from anything that could be associated with such behavior. They speak endlessly of God's mercy but not of his justice, forgetting that without justice there can be no mercy. Both are attributes of godliness, and no gospel system can exist without the perfect union of the two. To suppose otherwise is akin to saying that God favors mercy but recognizes no evil and that nothing is deserving of punishment. God simply cannot be broad-minded about evil. He cannot tolerate sin in the least degree. My experience, and I am sure it is not unlike that of others, is that those who profess to be the most broad-minded are very intolerant of those who do not share their broad-mindedness. Everything is acceptable to them save that which says that everything is not acceptable.

Those who are offended with the idea of doctrine seek to convince us that all that really matters is that we love one another and are gracious and charitable in all our relationships. To oppose such notions is like opposing motherhood and apple pie. No right thinking person is against love, charity, or the importance of living by Christlike standards. Nevertheless, such expressions represent a loss of spiritual focus. If love and charity have the power of salvation in them, then why the necessity of Christ and his atoning sacrifice? Why did Joseph and Hyrum Smith die in Carthage? Why were the heavens opened and angels sent to earth to restore keys and authority? What is the necessity of the ordinances of salvation? What is the purpose of temples? Why do we need scriptures and living prophets?

Paul said that if we have not charity, we are as sounding brass and as a tinkling cymbal, but that does not discount Christ's saying we must be baptized or be damned. That is hard doctrine. There is no compromise in it. It is an expression of belief out of which behavior is to grow. Proper behavior does not float around like a ship at sea without a rudder. Good doctrine must be the rudder for good behavior. All who live a kindly life will be richly rewarded by our eternal Father, but only those who are valiant in the testimony will be exalted. To be valiant in testimony is to be valiant in behavior that builds the kingdom of God. To advocate a position that does not sustain the need for the doctrines and discipline of the church Christ organized is something less than valiant.

There have always been those who claim membership in the Church while seeking to change its doctrines for one purpose or another. Such people generally like labels and refer to themselves as intellectuals or liberals. Responding to the spirit of such, Elder John A. Widtsoe observed: "The self-called liberal is one who has broken with the fundamental principles or guiding philosophy to which he belongs. He is an unbeliever. He claims membership in an organization but does not believe in its basic concepts and sets out to reform it by changing its foundations. He is forever entangling his unbelief with his membership. He wants the protection of the organization and, therefore, admits frankly that he rejects the fundamental beliefs of the cause and seeks truth elsewhere. It is a species of cowardice. In a Church the liberal refuses to accept the doctrine of the Church or the way of life it enjoins upon its members. It is undeserved compliments to designate by the noble word of liberal. They are apostates from a cause, engaged in building their own cause under false convictions, rudderless mariners, victims of every passing wave. Such men whatever they may call themselves are dangerous to human happiness. Certainly they are not entitled to be called liberals within the organization in which they are members. Their chief pastime is to sow the seeds of anarchy in the hearts of others. It is folly to speak of a liberal religion if that religion claims to and rests upon unchanging truth.

"It is well to beware of people who go about proclaiming that they are or their churches are liberal. The probabilities are that the structure of their faith is built on sand and will not withstand the storms of truth."[9]

THOSE WHO WOULD DEPART FROM THE GOSPEL

In like manner Elder Spencer W. Kimball described the pattern common to those who leave the Church to become cultists. He noted that they seldom direct their attention to doctrine at first but more often to the failings of our leaders. "They who garnish the sepulchers of the dead prophets begin now by stoning the living ones. They return to the pronouncements of the dead leaders and interpret them to be incompatible with present programs. They convince themselves that there are discrepancies between the practices of the deceased and the leaders of the present. . . .

"Apply this to modern times and you have the so-called reformers. Many budding apostates follow the pattern progressively. They allege love for the gospel and the Church but charge that leaders are a little 'off the beam'! Soon they claim that the leaders are making changes and not following the original programs. Next they say that while the gospel and the Church are divine, the leaders are fallen. Up to this time it may be a passive thing, but now it becomes an active resistance and frequently the blooming apostate begins to air his views and to crusade. He is likely now to join groups who are slipping away. He may become a student of the *Journal of Discourses* and is flattered by the evil one that he knows more about the scriptures and doctrines than the Church leaders who, he says, are now persecuting him. He generally wants all the blessings of the Church: membership, its Priesthood, its temple privileges, and expects them from the leaders of the Church, though at the same time claiming that those same leaders have departed from the path. He now begins to expect persecution and adopts a martyr complex, and when finally excommunication comes he associates himself with other apostates to develop or strengthen cults. At this stage he is likely to claim revelation for himself; revelations from the Lord directing him in his interpretations and his actions. Those manifestations are superior to anything from living leaders, he claims. He is now becoming quite independent."[10]

COMPETENT WITNESSES

All doctrines have a spirit innate to themselves. That spirit testifies of their truthfulness. Thus everyone who lives a gospel principle will through that association know, by the witness of the Spirit, the truthfulness of the principle. For instance, through the payment of an honest tithe, one gains a testimony of the principle of tithing; by living the Word of Wisdom, one obtains a testimony of the Word of Wisdom. Every member of the Church is expected to be a living witness of its doctrines because they live them and because they have received the witness of the Spirit. Thus no one need lean on borrowed light, for all are entitled to both witnesses. All must stand as competent witnesses of the faith.

The vitality of our faith is found in its doctrines. Those doctrines have engendered a faith that is unmatched in all the world. As a people, we have passed through much bigotry and persecution. As the gospel message goes to the nations of the earth, we have every expectation that we will yet see more of the same. Were our doctrines untrue, the world would let us alone. The devil doesn't bother to kick a dead dog. Validity draws the fire.

Moroni told Joseph Smith, then an uneducated seventeen-year-old boy, that his name would be had for good and evil among all the peoples of the earth (Joseph Smith–History 1:33). It is a most remarkable prophecy. Fourteen years later, while Joseph Smith was incarcerated in the Liberty Jail, the Lord affirmed that prophecy, saying: "The ends of the earth shall inquire after thy name, and fools shall have thee in derision, and hell shall rage against thee; while the pure in heart, and the wise, and the noble, and the virtuous, shall seek counsel, and authority, and blessings constantly from under thy hand" (D&C 122:1–2).

Our destiny as a people is to take that message restored through the Prophet Joseph Smith to the ends of the earth. We echo the testimony of the Prophet. As our testimony is the same and our doctrines the same, our experiences in bearing that testimony will be the same. Some will hold us in honor; others in derision. Such is our destiny, as it has been the destiny of the children of God in all ages of earth's history. So be it.

Our faith is not predicated on the concurrence of sectarian scholarship. As to the saving principles of the gospel of Jesus Christ, we have been sent forth to teach, not to be taught (D&C 43:15). The Savior is our exemplar; of him we read, "And he served under his father, and he spake not as other men, neither could he be taught: for he needed not that any man should teach him" (JST Matthew 3:25).

Whether they agree or disagree with us has nothing in the world to do with why we believe or disbelieve a particular thing. For us to court the world's approval or to attempt to sustain our faith because sources respectable in the world agree with us is, at best, shortsighted. Surely, we would not abandon a doctrine because those not of our faith did not accept it. Further, great care should be taken in quoting those not of our faith for the purpose of sustaining our faith. If those we quote were truly in agreement with us, why have they not numbered themselves among us?

NOTES

1. See Peter Widdicombe, *The Fatherhood of God from Origen to Athanasius* (Oxford: Clarendon Press, 1994), pp. 15–18. See also Joseph Fielding McConkie, *Sons and Daughters of God: The Loss and Restoration of Our Divine Inheritance* (Salt Lake City: Bookcraft, 1994), pp. 109–11.

2. Bruce R. McConkie, *The Foolishness of Teaching,* address delivered to seminary and institute teachers (Salt Lake City: The Church of Jesus Christ of Latter-day Saints, 1981), p. 4.

3. J. Reuben Clark Jr., *The Charted Course of the Church in Education,* address delivered to seminary and institute teachers, Aspen Grove, Utah, 8 Aug. 1938, p. 6; also in McConkie, *Foolishness of Teaching,* p. 5.

4. Joseph Smith, *Teachings of the Prophet Joseph Smith,* sel. Joseph Fielding Smith (Salt Lake City: Deseret Book, 1974), pp. 166–67.

5. Brigham Young, *Discourses of Brigham Young,* sel. John A. Widtsoe (Salt Lake City: Deseret Book, 1954), p. 338.

6. Robert L. Millet, "'Praise to the Man': Loyalty to the Prophet Joseph Smith," in *Regional Studies in Latter-day Saint History: Illinois,* ed. H. Dean Garrett (Provo, Utah: Department of Church History and Doctrine, Brigham Young University, 1995), pp. 9–10.

7. Millet, "'Praise to the Man,'" p. 10.

8. Joseph F. Smith, *Gospel Doctrine* (Salt Lake City: Deseret Book, 1986), p. 373.

9. John A. Widtsoe, as quoted by Harold B. Lee, *Viewpoint of a Giant,* address delivered to seminary and institute teachers, Provo, Utah, 18 July 1968, pp. 3–4.

10. Spencer W. Kimball, *That You May Not Be Deceived,* Brigham Young University Speeches of the Year, Provo, Utah, 11 Nov. 1959, pp. 5–6.

Chapter Eight

ONE TRUE CHURCH

Behold there are save two churches only; the one is the church of the Lamb of God, and the other is the church of the devil; wherefore, whoso belongeth not to the church of the Lamb of God belongeth to that great church, which is the mother of abominations; and she is the whore of all the earth.

—1 Nephi 14:10

IN A DISCUSSION OF religious issues few questions are more emotionally charged than that of whether there is only one true church. The announcement that only one church can be true, with its attendant implication that all others are false, gives immediate offense to many who suppose that such a conclusion excludes great hosts of wonderful people from the love of God and the blessings of heaven. It is thought to be incompatible with the idea of a loving God and often is labeled as both intolerant and unchristian. Thus it is essential to respond to this issue.

Are there false churches? The answer to the question, Are there false churches? is less threatening than the answer to the question, Is there only one true church? It would generally be agreed that just as there are false ideas, so there are false churches. Certainly the Bible speaks of false teachers, false prophets, and even false Christs. It would also be agreed among thoughtful people that no real blessings can accrue from falsehoods. To mistakenly swallow poison makes it no less harmful than taking it by design. Surely there are ideas that are as harmful to the soul as there are practices that are harmful to the mortal body.

Why would we suppose that there is but one true church? Perhaps it ought be asked, Is there law in the universe, law that governs all things? Must we discover and obey this law to obtain the desired results? If that be so, are there any fields that can be excepted from this principle, fields governed by chaos rather than law? Suppose, for instance, a dozen people add a column of figures and each arrives at a different sum—can all twelve be right? Suppose a dozen chemists set out to make a specified substance, and suppose also that they all attempt it by using different materials. How many of their number will succeed? Let us add another element and suppose that the people involved are very sincere. Can that in some way change things?

We need further ask, Could the nature of our universe be such that law governs all save that which is spiritual? Could it be that in the realm of spiritual things chaos governs? Could it be that in some instances wickedness does bring happiness and in others it does not and that there is no way for us to know what the result of our particular actions will be? If there are eternal laws, could it be that God has left it to each man, woman, and child to determine for himself which of those laws will apply to him and which will not? Is salvation simply a divine smorgasbord at which we all satisfy our own appetites, or would it be more true to all we know and have experienced to conclude that there are spiritual laws, just as there are temporal laws, and that "when we obtain any blessing from God, it is by obedience to that law upon which it is predicated"? (D&C 130:21).

If such principles as righteousness, peace, and order are to be found in heaven, then it must be a kingdom governed by laws; and if there are such laws, then there must be a right and proper path that leads the soul back to the presence of the Father and all must follow the same path, just as all must follow the same laws to obtain results in the physical world of which we are a part.

Does the idea that there are spiritual laws that must be lived in order to receive the blessings of heaven make God unloving or unjust? Quite the opposite. The knowledge that there is a sure path and all are invited to travel it assures us of God's universal love and of his unfailing justice. A doctor cannot respond to the plea of his sick patient by saying, "Take whatever medicine you want. Whatever you choose to do will be just fine." Nor can we expect the God of heaven to respond to the distraught soul by saying, "Oh, any church will do; choose your own plan of salvation—whatever you do will bless you." If we are going to argue that such a response from God is evidence of his love, then we must also argue that such a response from a physician is evidence of his concern for his patient.

Singularly, it is in the doctrine that there is but one true church that we find the perfect manifestation of God's love and his justice. The notion that salvation can be found by following any path of one's choosing negates the need for a Savior, for obedience, or for righteousness. It does away with the need for faith and for religion in any organized form. It excuses us from any responsibility one for another and suggests that God couldn't care less. It further suggests that to be good parents we ought to let our own children run wild. After all, to discipline them to a single standard, as the argument goes, would be unchristian.

Is a church organization necessary? No one ever started life in this world fully grown, and never has there been an infant child that survived to adulthood without the protecting care of others. The human race survives only because of its willingness to help one another. The more advanced and productive the society, the greater its interdependency. As it is in the realm of temporal things, so it is in the realm of spiritual things. No one commences life spiritually mature. All, the Son of God included, are required to advance from grace to grace in order to receive the fulness of the Father (see D&C 93:6–18). We would all be impoverished if we could read no books save those we had written, hear no music save that which we composed, played no instruments except those we made, hear no sermons except those we preached, and follow no example except our own. We are all in need of spiritual mentors, just as we are all in need of teachers in the temporal realm. We do not perform the ordinances of salvation for ourselves, nor do we determine our own worthiness to receive them. It is through the organization of the Church that the principles of salvation are taught both to those within the fold and those without.

What is the church? The true church is the kingdom of God on earth, and as such has an organization, officers to administer its affairs, and principles upon which it operates. Jesus the Christ is its heavenly King, and the senior apostle of God on earth serves as the presiding officer in this mortal sphere. He receives direction and guidance from the heavenly King by the power of the Holy Ghost. The church is thus an organized body of true believers; it is composed of those who believe the gospel and seek salvation by obedience to its laws and ordinances. Because of the atonement of Christ, all who seek salvation may obtain it by obedience to the laws and ordinances of the gospel. Thus there neither is nor can be salvation outside the true church.

As the gospel is everlasting and eternal, so is the Lord's church. It has existed in all earthly gospel dispensations. It was the church in the days of Melchizedek that named the holy priesthood after that great high priest (see D&C 107:4). The Book of Mormon frequently mentions the church in what historical Christianity presumes is the pre-Christian era. Most of what we know of church organization and functioning comes from the New Testament era. Those who obtain exaltation will be members of the Church of the Firstborn in the celestial world.

Just as the gospel is the Lord's, so the church that administers it must be his also. He must be its creator, the source of its power and authority. It must teach his laws, his ordinances, and his doctrines. He must direct its affairs, even from day to day. Such a church could not exist without the Spirit of revelation, meaning ongoing and continuous revelation suited to each particular time and season through which his church must pass. The organization thus established remains his church as long as it follows his direction and stays on the course he has charted. His earthly servants, those called to administer in his name, are to say and do what he himself would say and do were he personally among us. Thus, if there is a true gospel and a true plan of salvation, there must of necessity be a true church to administer the same.

Is the gospel the same in all ages? Inherent in the verity that there is but one true church, one path to the presence of our eternal Father, is the assurance that the gospel is the same in all ages of earth's history and among all peoples. Eternal principles are as fixed and sure as the God from whence they came. If, as holy writ declares, God is the same yesterday, today, and forever; if he is a holy being in whom there is no variability, neither shadow of turning; and if souls have been equally precious in his sight in all ages—then his saving power could not be, as traditional Christianity tells us it is—restricted to the so-called Christian era. Could a just God deny the blessings of salvation to Adam, Enoch, Noah, or any other righteous soul who lived before the Flood? Could he deny the fulness of gospel blessings to Abraham, Isaac, and Jacob, or any of their righteous contemporaries? And what of the host of Israel, his own peculiar people? Did he give them prophets but not the gospel? In writing upon the tables with his own finger, did he forget to tell them that salvation was in the name of Christ and none other? Are we to assume that such a determination had not yet been made in the heavens?

Was it not an angel from heaven who declared to John that the gospel of Christ is an "everlasting gospel"? (Revelation 14:6). As such, it has found place in the hearts and souls of the faithful in all ages and at all times. It has been dispensed from God in heaven to man on earth in a series of great dispensations. Those dispensations constitute the occasions when the plan of salvation is revealed anew through living prophets so that those of that dispensation would stand independent of that which had been given previously. This system of gospel dispensations began with Adam, the first man and primal parent of the human race. In his day the proclamation went forth that men should worship the Lord their God and him only should they serve, and that they should "believe on his Only Begotten Son, even him whom he declared should come in the meridian of time, who was prepared from before the foundation of the world." So it was that "the Gospel began to be preached, from the beginning, being declared by holy angels sent forth from the presence of God, and by his own voice, and by the gift of the Holy Ghost. And thus all things were confirmed unto Adam, by an holy ordinance, and the Gospel preached, and a decree sent forth, that it should be in the world, until the end thereof" (Moses 5:58–59).

Adam, Enoch, and Noah each in turn received a dispensation of the gospel. Enoch was one of the greatest preachers of righteousness ever to dwell on earth. Noah stood as a pillar of truth and righteousness in the midst of a wicked and evil generation ripening for destruction. "And the Lord ordained Noah after his own order, and commanded him that he should go forth and declare his Gospel unto the children of men, even as it was given unto Enoch." The message Noah proclaimed to the worldly people of his day was "believe and repent of your sins and be baptized in the name of Jesus Christ, the Son of God, even as our fathers, and ye shall receive the Holy Ghost, that ye may have all things made manifest" (Moses 8:19, 24).

Paul tells us that "God . . . preached before the gospel unto Abraham" (Galatians 3:8) and that "unto us [those who lived in the meridian day] was the gospel preached, as well as unto them [Israel in the day of Moses]: but the word preached did not profit them, not being mixed with faith in them that heard it" (Hebrews 4:2). Indeed, Paul testifies that "therein [the gospel, which is the power of God unto salvation] is the righteousness of God revealed from faith to faith: as it is written, the just shall live by faith" (Romans 1:16–17). In other words, from age to age, whenever there were just men and women on earth, the Lord gave them his everlasting gospel to enable them to live by faith.

Where among all the churches of Christendom is it known and taught that the everlasting gospel has been given to men in a series of dispensations? Who among them knows that when Jesus came among the Jews, teaching that which his Father commanded him, he was restoring what had been lost by apostasy? Can any church be true that does not believe and teach that the gospel of salvation, the gospel of the Everlasting God, is itself the everlasting word of truth and salvation?

Is the organization of the Lord's church the same in all ages? As we have just seen, the principles of salvation must be everlastingly the same. The organization through which they are administered, however, can and may change. Its principles are eternal and as such are irrevocable; its policies, on the other hand, are not, and thus they properly may change as circumstances change. For example, in the early part of the Old Testament, the organization of the Church was familial. When the nation of Israel was formed, the organization of the Church became much more complex. Similarly, when the Church was organized for the first time in this dispensation, it had only a handful of members and a correspondingly simple organizational structure. Today, with millions of members, that organization is appreciably more complex, and it will, of course, continue to grow and change. Nevertheless, we will always be able to describe the Church as Joseph Smith did in the sixth Article of Faith: "We believe in the same organization that existed in the Primitive Church, namely, apostles, prophets, pastors, teachers, evangelists, and so forth."

Is there a church of the devil? There has always been a church of the devil. Wherever and whenever the truths of salvation are proclaimed, Joseph Smith taught us, then the devil "always sets up his kingdom" in opposition to the kingdom of God.[1] The devil first organized his church in the premortal existence. Its purpose was to oppose the plan of salvation established by the Great Elohim and to substitute for it a devilish proposal to save all men by denying them their agency. Lucifer's proposition meant salvation without righteousness, without testing, and without progression. The members of his church came out in open rebellion against God in our first estate, in consequence of which there was war in heaven. Lucifer and his legions were cast out, losing the privilege of obtaining bodies in this mortal probation. Thus they became *perdition,* which means hopelessly lost.

The devil and his church existed in the days of Adam. Cain, who "loved Satan" and entered into covenants with him, became its first prophet. When Adam and Eve taught their children that salvation was in Christ and in the Atonement he would bring to pass, "Satan came among them, saying: I am also a son of God; and he commanded them, saying: Believe it [the gospel of Christ] not; and they believed it not, and they loved Satan more than God. And [the posterity of Adam] began from that time forth to be carnal, sensual, and devilish," signifying that they loved Satan more than God, and thus they have chosen to be citizens of his church and kingdom (Moses 5:13).

Our concern, however, is not with the church of the devil and its various sects, cults, and branches as they existed in the day before the coming of the Son of God in the flesh. Rather, we need be concerned with the organization, doctrines, ordinances, and system of worship of that church in our day. John the Revelator, in Revelation 17 and 18, tells us of the fall of this great church, which is destined to occur when the Lord comes to usher in the millennial reign. John designates the church as "MYSTERY, BABYLON THE GREAT, THE MOTHER OF HARLOTS AND ABOMINATIONS OF THE EARTH" (Revelation 17:5). He tells of her evils and iniquities, of her sorceries that deceived nations, of the blood of prophets and Saints that drenches her hands, and of how she made merchandise of the souls of men. These two chapters of holy writ are deserving of careful and attentive study.

But for this discussion let us take the similar passage found in the Book of Mormon. It has the advantage of being accurately placed in its proper historical setting. Nephi foresaw the ministry of John the Baptist; the birth, ministry, and crucifixion of the Son of God; and the persecutions that were heaped upon the Twelve Apostles of the Lamb (1 Nephi 11:27–36). Then, after all this, he saw the formation of the church of the devil among the Gentile nations, which were separated from the Americas by many waters (1 Nephi 13–14).

"I saw among the nations of the Gentiles the formation of a great church." That occurred after the days of the original Twelve. "And the angel said unto me: Behold the formation of a church which is most abominable above all other churches, which slayeth the saints of God, yea, and tortureth them and bindeth them down, and yoketh them with a yoke of iron, and bringeth them down into captivity" (1 Nephi 13:4–5). There are many abominable churches, many that run counter to the mind and will of the Lord, many that teach false doctrines in which there is no salvation; but there is one that ranks as the most abominable of them all.

"And it came to pass that I beheld this great and abominable church"—the one that is more depraved and devilish than any of the others—"and I saw the devil that he was the founder of it." He may be the founder of them all, but more of his influence and more of his evil ways are manifest in this particular church than in any of the others. "And I also saw gold, and silver, and silks, and scarlets, and fine-twined linen, and all manner of precious clothing; and I saw many harlots. And the angel spake unto me, saying: Behold the gold, and the silver, and the silks, and the scarlets, and the fine-twined linen, and the precious clothing, and the harlots, are the desires of this great and abominable church. And also for the praise of the world do they destroy the saints of God, and bring them down into captivity" (1 Nephi 13:6–9).

A few verses later, Nephi again uses the word *harlot* to describe apostasy from the truth. The "abominable church," he says, "is the mother of harlots," meaning that the great and abominable church spawns daughter churches, also apostate in their nature, which are also likened unto harlots (1 Nephi 13:34). And he also saw the perversion of the Bible in an earlier age by the great and abominable church, which caused mankind to stumble and fall away from the true gospel.

Then Nephi saw the day of restoration, in which we live. "And it shall come to pass, that if the Gentiles shall hearken unto the Lamb of God in that day that he shall manifest himself unto them in word, and also in power, in very deed, unto the taking away of their stumbling blocks" (1 Nephi 14:1), they shall be marvelously blessed. That is, if the Gentiles, in the latter days, in the day of the restoration of the gospel, shall hearken unto the Lord, he will remove the stumbling block of a perverted Bible by giving them the Book of Mormon and other latter-day revelations, and they shall be numbered with the blessed ones in the house of Israel. Then "that great pit, which hath been digged for them by that great and abominable church, which was founded by the devil and his children, that he might lead away the souls of men down to hell—yea, that great pit which hath been digged for the destruction of men shall be filled by those who digged it, unto their utter destruction" (1 Nephi 14:3).

Then, of the Restoration, of the day when the Lord will have done "a great and a marvelous work among the children of men," the angel said to Nephi, "Look, and behold that great and abominable church, which is the mother of abominations, whose founder is the devil" (1 Nephi 14:7, 9). This time Nephi sees not one church in particular that ranks as the most abominable of all churches but rather all false churches lumped together under the one flag of abomination.

These are the angelic words describing churches in the day of the restoration of the gospel: "Behold there are save two churches only; the one is the church of the Lamb of God, and the other is the church of the devil." This could not have been said of earlier days, for the true church, once lost through apostasy, was now restored. "Wherefore, whoso belongeth to that great church, which is the mother of abominations; and she is the whore of all the earth" (1 Nephi 14:10).

Nephi, recording what he saw of our day, said: "And it came to pass that I looked and beheld the whore of all the earth, and she sat upon many waters; and she had dominion over all the earth, among all nations, kindreds, tongues, and people" (1 Nephi 14:11). This evil church is thus an organization composed of all false churches, of all evil powers, of everything that is carnal, sensual, and devilish. All of these are part and parcel of the church of the devil, for their power is not to prepare mankind for heaven but to send them to hell.

"And it came to pass that I beheld the church of the Lamb of God, and its numbers were few, because of the wickedness and abominations of the whore who sat upon many waters; nevertheless, I beheld that the church of the Lamb, who were the saints of God, were also upon all the face of the earth; and their dominions upon the face of the earth were small, because of the wickedness of the great whore whom I saw" (1 Nephi 14:12). Nephi then saw the wars and desolations that would result from the warfare between the Saints of God and the worldliness of Babylon, with the wrath of God being poured out upon all that is evil, wicked, and degenerate.

"And when the day cometh that the wrath of God is poured out upon the mother of harlots, which is the great and abominable church of all the earth, whose founder is the devil, then, at that day, the work of the Father shall commence, in preparing the way for the fulfilling of his covenants, which he hath made to his people who are of the house of Israel" (1 Nephi 14:17).

Finally, after giving assurance that the Lord "will preserve the righteous by his power" in the last days, Nephi summarizes the state of all the sects, cults, and branches of the church of the devil: "The time speedily shall come that all churches which are built up to get gain, and all those who are built up to get power over the flesh, and those who are built up to become popular in the eyes of the world, and those who seek the lusts of the flesh and the things of the world, and to do all manner of iniquity; yea, in fine, all those who belong to the kingdom of the devil are they who need fear, and tremble, and quake; they are those who must be brought low in the dust; they are those who must be consumed as stubble" (1 Nephi 22:17, 23).

We are left, then, with the sure witness, taught in the holy word, that the kingdom of the devil has many churches, some of which are more abominable than others, and that each one standing alone, as well as all of them combined, constitute the church of the devil.

Are there churches of men? Are there churches that have been founded by honorable men for uplifting purposes? Are there churches that have a mellowing effect on the hearts of individuals, that teach honesty, chastity, charity, and good family values? Are there churches that teach a reverence for the Bible? Are there churches that teach Jesus of Nazareth as the promised Messiah, the source of salvation? The answer is an unhesitating yes. Yet, as already noted, Nephi testified that "there are save two churches only; the one is the church of the Lamb of God, and the other is the church of the devil; wherefore, whoso belongeth not to the church of the Lamb of God belongeth to that great church, which is the mother of abominations; and she is the whore of all the earth" (1 Nephi 14:10). The context of Nephi's division of churches into one of two camps, those belonging to the Lamb of God and those who are disciples of the devil, comes only after the Church of Jesus Christ was restored in April of 1830. Before that time, many courageous and honorable people had bound themselves together in various church organizations to search for freedom of worship and for greater light and knowledge. In many cases such churches did the work of an Elias in preparing the way for the restored gospel and in so doing represented the inspiration of heaven (see D&C 35:4). Like the disciples of John the Baptist, who left him to follow the Christ, the members of such churches, if they truly have the Spirit of Christ, will respond to the fulness of the gospel message when it is presented to them. A classic illustration is the preachers gathered at Benbow's farm under the title United Brethren, to whom Wilford Woodruff preached the Restoration with such great effect. Nevertheless, when the members of the churches of men have a greater sense of loyalty to their own traditions than to the truths of salvation and thus reject the fulness of the gospel when it is brought to them, they are working a great evil. There is no neutrality on such matters. We either get on the good ship Zion or we are left behind. The favorite litany of those left behind is "We have the Bible, and that is sufficient for us." Thus in the false security of the doctrine of sufficiency, they reject living prophets in a misguided reverence for those who are dead.

Those who argue in defense of the churches of men cite the good things they have done, asking, Could God disapprove of that? No, he does not disapprove of any good work. But that is the wrong question. The questions that need to be asked are, Do individuals who have done good works have the power to resurrect themselves? Do their good works grant them the power to remit their own sins or to create their own celestial kingdom? Can they ordain laws that will assure themselves or others glory in such kingdoms? In short, can a person save himself? It would be well for all to be reminded that "everything that is in the world, whether it be ordained of men, by thrones, or principalities, or powers, or things of name, whatsoever they may be, that are not by me or by my word, saith the Lord, shall be thrown down, and shall not remain after men are dead, neither in nor after the resurrection, saith the Lord your God, for whatsoever things remain are by me; and whosoever things are not by me shall be shaken and destroyed" (D&C 132:13–14).

Can faith be found in other than the true church? Faith cannot be exercised in principles that are false. No amount of faith can turn a falsehood into a truth or allow the unrepentant soul place in the kingdom of God. Speaking of the wickedness of his people, Mormon lamented that he had led them into battle many times "and had loved them, according to the love of God which was in me, with all my heart; and my soul had been poured out in prayer unto my God all the day long for them; nevertheless, it was without faith, because of the hardness of their hearts" (Mormon 3:12). Using the sacrifices of Cain and Abel to teach this principle, Joseph Smith explained: "By faith in this atonement or plan of redemption, Abel offered to God a sacrifice that was accepted, which was the firstlings of the flock.

Cain offered of the fruit of the ground, and was not accepted, because he could not do it in faith, he could have no faith, or could not exercise faith contrary to the plan of heaven. It must be shedding the blood of the Only Begotten to atone for man; for this was the plan of redemption; and without the shedding of blood was no remission; and as the sacrifice was instituted for a type, by which man was to discern the great Sacrifice which God had prepared; to offer a sacrifice contrary to that, no faith could be exercised, because redemption was not purchased in that way, nor the power of atonement instituted after that order; consequently Cain could have no faith; and whatsoever is not of faith, is sin."[2] Alma said, "Faith is not to have a perfect knowledge of things; therefore if ye have faith ye hope for things which are not seen, which are true" (Alma 32:21).

To pray to a god concocted from the speculations of philosophers is no different from praying to a god carved from wood or chiseled from stone. Ten thousand times ten thousand prayers cannot confer any authority upon it. To suppose otherwise would bring all the heavens into a chaotic state, making falsehood of equal worth with truth and rewarding sin the same as righteousness.

Can faith be found outside the Church of Jesus Christ? Certainly it can be found anywhere we can also find the truths of heaven. We can exercise faith only to the extent that we are in possession of those truths. That is why membership in the Church becomes so important. The Church is the school and its curriculum is the principles out of which faith grows.

WHAT ARE THE CHARACTERISTICS OF THE TRUE CHURCH?

Name

The name of the Church is among the plain and precious things lost from the Bible record. The word *church* cannot even be found in the Old Testament. Though the necessity of a church organization is acknowledged in the New Testament, the name of the Church is not given. The Book of Mormon announces the matter in plainness. The Nephite Twelve asked Christ: "Lord, we will that thou wouldst tell us the name whereby we shall call this church." His response included a mild rebuke. Had they not read the scriptures, which say one must take upon one the name of Christ? Then he reasoned with them, saying: "For by this name shall ye be called at the last day; and whoso taketh upon him my name, and endureth to the end, the same shall be saved at the last day. Therefore, whatsoever ye shall do, ye shall do it in my name; therefore ye shall call the church in my name; and ye shall call upon the Father in my name that he will bless the church for my sake" (3 Nephi 27:3, 5–6). Now we might ask, How could a person truly take upon himself the name of Christ unless he were a member of a church that bears his name?

The Savior continued: "And how be it my church save it be called in my name? For if a church be called in Moses' name then it be Moses' church; or if it be called in the name of a man then it be the church of a man; but if it be called in my name then it is my church, if it so be that they are built upon my gospel. Verily I say unto you, that ye are built upon my gospel; therefore ye shall call whatsoever things ye do call, in my name; therefore if ye call upon the Father, for the church, if it be in my name the Father will hear you" (3 Nephi 27:8–9).

In this dispensation the Church was formally named The Church of Jesus Christ of Latter-day Saints by revelation on April 26, 1838 (D&C 115:4).

Authority in the Ministry

From whence comes the right or authority to speak for the Lord? Is it the rightful province of any man or woman who feels moved upon to do so? Does it come from reading the Bible? Can it be granted by a college or seminary to its graduating class? Should the answer be found in such suggestions, then God has surrendered control of his kingdom both in heaven and on earth and the church may well become a refuge for scoundrels and rogues. Surely it is for the Lord to choose who will speak for him, and it is also for him to tell them precisely what they are to say. "Behold, mine house is a house of order, saith the Lord God, and not a house of confusion. Will I accept of an offering, saith the Lord, that is not made in my name? Or will I receive at your hands that which I have not appointed? And will I appoint unto you, saith the Lord, except it be by law, even as I and my Father ordained unto you, before the world was?" (D&C 132:8–11).

Priesthood and Keys

Priesthood, that is, the authority to act in the name of the Lord, cannot be had by any who do not believe in revelation that is immediate to the circumstance at hand. One cannot profess to be God's agent on the one hand and on the other to teach that God has quit speaking. As there can be no priesthood without revelation, so there can be no priesthood without order. The principle that brings order and discipline to the priesthood is known as the keys, or the keys of the kingdom. The keys are the right of presidency, meaning the authority of one to preside and give direction to all who hold the priesthood. Thus all who hold the priesthood will always be found functioning according to the laws of heaven. That requires, as do all organizations, a system of rank and authority.

Doctrines

The issue of pure doctrine—its nature and source—having been discussed in the previous chapter, it will suffice at this point to say that to be true, a church must be the source of the knowledge of the plan of salvation for all the inhabitants of the earth. Thus we find the Lord telling the Prophet Joseph Smith, "This greater priesthood [that is, the Melchizedek Priesthood] administereth the gospel and holdeth the key of the mysteries of the kingdom, even the key of the knowledge of God" (D&C 84:19). One distinguishing feature of the plan of salvation is that it must be everlastingly the same. It is not like a product that we bid for in the market place whose cost may rise or fall. It cannot be granted in one dispensation by grace alone and at the cost of exacting discipleship to those of another. The law of the gospel and the ordinances of salvation must be one and the same for all the sons and daughters of God.

The law of the gospel is administered by covenant, and thus the Lord's people always have been and always will be a covenant people. For instance, all must enter into the covenant of baptism, and all must endure in faith to the end, "not only those who believed after he came in the meridian of time, in the flesh, but all those from the beginning, even as many as were before he came, who believed in the words of the holy prophets, who spake as they were inspired by the gift of the Holy Ghost, who truly testified of him in all things, should have eternal life, as well as those who should come after, who should believe in the gifts and callings of God by the Holy Ghost, which beareth record of the Father and of the Son; which Father, Son, and Holy Ghost are one God, infinite and eternal, without end" (D&C 20:26–28).

A true and living church will be in continuous communion with the God of heaven. Could you imagine a marriage in which one of the partners was expected to record what the other one said in the early years of their marriage and then let that written word suffice as communication for the rest of the relationship? Could you imagine parents who chose to communicate with only one of their children, who in turn was expected to record what they said and pass it on to the other children with the explanation that what had been written was sufficient for them also? As to prophets, they are to the church what inspired parents are to a family. The knowledge of the goodness of my great-grandparents will never replace the need my teenage children have for parents of their own.

A church that does not respect the sanctity of agency, seeking to impose its will by the sword, by inquisition, or by an alliance with the governments of men, has no claim on either the love of God or the authority of heaven. The powers of heaven must rest upon principles of righteousness. "No power or influence can or ought to be maintained by virtue of the priesthood, only by persuasion, by long-suffering, by gentleness and meekness, and by love unfeigned; by kindness, and pure knowledge" (D&C 121:41–42).

A church that does not actively assume the responsibility to take the message of salvation to the ends of the earth, to every nation, kindred, and tongue, cannot even for a moment suppose itself to be the legitimate representative of the God of heaven. To say otherwise would be to make God a respecter of persons, the creator of races not entitled to the fulness of his blessings, and rob him of any pretense to justice. Of necessity the God of heaven will have a divine timetable by which the fulness of his gospel will reach out to each and every soul, but that all must have a full and equal chance before the Day of Judgment is beyond refutation. Implied in such an announcement is the doctrine of teaching the gospel in the world of departed spirits, those souls who have lived and died without the opportunity to embrace its truths in this mortal sphere. I once had a discussion with two ministers of another faith. They roundly denounced Mormonism as a heresy and condemned me to the lowest depths of hell. I asked if salvation could be found only in their brand of theology. They assured me that such was the case. I pointed out to them that since the Second World War II more than a billion people had lived and died without hearing their message. What of them, I asked? To which the response was "Well, that's their tough luck, isn't it!"

Could you imagine God responding in such a manner? The Bible, for which these men profess such a love, tells us that a sparrow does not fall save he knows it and that a hair cannot fall from our heads without his knowledge of it, and yet these ministers would have us believe that he has no provision in the gospel plan to teach the greater part of his own family! In such a theology, the system of salvation resembles a lottery more than the plan of a loving Father seeking the interest of his children.

The Church of Jesus Christ must always be distinguishable by the fruits of faith, for faith is an anchor to the soul and makes those who possess it "sure and steadfast, always abounding in good works, being led to glorify God" (Ether 12:4). Thus there will always be sure signs that follow them that believe. Those signs will include dreams, visions, revelations, the ministration of angels, the working of miracles, healings, and all manner of wonderful works. They will also include apostles, and prophets, and the same gifts and powers that existed in the Primitive Church (see D&C 84:64–73).[3]

THE DISCIPLINE OF DISCIPLESHIP

The arguments against the doctrine that declares that there can be only one true church reduce themselves to a rejection of the discipline associated with true discipleship. Such arguments are popular among those professing a loyalty to the gospel cause while having no intention of enlisting in the army of the Lord. As to the straight and narrow path, they talk it but do not walk it.

To suppose that the church you are a member of doesn't matter is to suppose that truth doesn't matter and that whoever chooses to do so can act in the name of the Lord, that it is for God to allow his kingdom to be taken over by others. It is also a rejection of the truth that the Lord's house is a house of order.

NOTES

1. Joseph Smith, *Teachings of the Prophet Joseph Smith,* sel. Joseph Fielding Smith (Salt Lake City: Deseret Book, 1974), p. 365.

2. Smith, *Teachings,* p. 58.

3. See also Joseph Smith, *Lectures on Faith* (Salt Lake City: Deseret Book, 1985), 7.20, pp. 82–83.

Chapter Nine

WE BELIEVE IN CHRIST

And we beheld the glory of the Son, on the right hand of the Father, and received of his fulness;

And saw the holy angels, and them who are sanctified before his throne, worshiping God, and the Lamb, who worship him forever and ever.

And now, after the many testimonies which have been given of him, this is the testimony, last of all, which we give of him: That he lives!

For we saw him, even on the right hand of God; and we heard the voice bearing record that he is the Only Begotten of the Father—

That by him, and through him, and of him, the worlds are and were created, and the inhabitants thereof are begotten sons and daughters unto God.

—Doctrine and Covenants 76:20–24

WE BELIEVE IN GOD, the Eternal Father, and in His Son, Jesus Christ, and in the Holy Ghost." Those words penned by the Prophet Joseph Smith are what is known today as the first of the

Articles of Faith. These thirteen single-sentence statements respond to often-asked questions about Latter-day Saint theology. The first article affirms our belief in the Father, the Son, and the Holy Ghost, but it does not detail the manner in which our belief differs from that of other professing Christians.

As Latter-day Saints we believe God to be a personal being possessing body, parts, and passions. We wholly reject the descriptions of him given in the creeds of Christendom and the philosophical speculations upon which those creeds are based. We claim the testimony of both the Father and the Son in declaring the dogmas of those creeds to be an abomination. The gospel dispensation of which we bear witness began with the appearance of God the Father and God the Son to the youthful Joseph Smith. Calling Joseph Smith by name, the Father introduced the Son: *"This is My Beloved Son. Hear Him!"* (Joseph Smith–History 1:17). The Savior instructed Joseph Smith not to join any of the churches of the day, saying that not only were their creeds an abomination but their "professors were all corrupt; that 'they draw near to me with their lips, but their hearts are far from me, they teach for doctrines the commandments of men, having a form of godliness, but they deny the power thereof'" (Joseph Smith–History 1:19).

THE LONG NIGHT OF APOSTATE DARKNESS

The creeds of Christendom are a perfect evidence of the apostasy. All Christian creeds trace themselves to Nicaea, where a great council of bishops met under the direction of the Roman Emperor Constantine, himself a sun worshipper. His desire was to unite his newly conquered kingdom, and he saw the Christian church as a means to that end. The difficulty was that Christianity was a host of squabbling factions, and he had first to bring unity to it. Primary among the issues of contention was the relationship between the

Father and the Son. To admit the existence of both was to offend the teachings of Plato, who had determined that the Good (to which Christians related as God) constituted the perfection of all things. His chain of thought held that there could be only one Absolute, and thus the idea of two gods was inconceivable. The Christian world had become so enamored of the philosophers' speculations that they viewed them as a pre-Christian Christianity. For the Council of Nicaea, it was monotheism at all cost and thus the decision of that assembly that Christ was his own Father. The result of such absurd reasoning, known to us today as the doctrine of the Holy Trinity, is covered with the explanation that it is a divine mystery. Athanasius, the great champion of this doctrine, explained "that reason must bow to the mystery of the Trinity."[1] It is not reason alone, however, that is offended by this doctrine. It also stands in contravention of countless passages in the Old and the New Testaments. This difficulty was resolved by declaring all positive affirmation about God in scripture to be metaphorical. Thus *The Cambridge History of the Bible* explains that "Eusebius [an early church apologist and theologian] is a faithful enough disciple of Origen [a partially converted pagan philosopher who labored to convince the church that God could have neither body or form] to agree with Plato that it is sometimes necessary for the lawgiver to lie in order to persuade people rather than coerce them, and to suggest that this is an explanation of the anthropomorphism of the Old Testament."[2] To the advocates of these creeds it is more acceptable to have a God who, in their language, "lies" than it is to suppose the scriptures actually mean what they say in their descriptions of him. By way of further explanation, *The Oxford Dictionary of the Christian Church* explains that "all affirmations of Scripture and the Fathers are but metaphors devised for the ignorant."[3]

Historical, or traditional, Christianity is founded on what traditional Christians themselves describe as a philosophical speculation.

It formally begins at Nicaea where scripture became the bride of philosophy in a wedding performed by the authority of Rome, a pagan state. The church in turn bound itself to the state. This union of Bible and sword marked the end of religious freedom for more than fourteen centuries, until the God of heaven would, according to prophecy, raise up a nation to reestablish it. Truths, once carried from heart to heart on the wings of the Spirit, were now supplanted by the dogma of creeds that forced mankind to kneel by the threat of an unsheathed sword. The church that once had been symbolized by love and light, was now housed in cold stone and dark naves. The dove that had been the sign of the Spirit's presence was replaced by the Roman cross of crucifixion.

The war against the testimony of Christ was as unremitting as the darkness of night. It allowed no hallowed place into which the light of heaven could shine. The apostles, those specially chosen to carry his name to the ends of the earth, were killed. We have been told that they died at the hands of heathens, but was it so? Consider carefully what Christ told them three days before his own death at the hands of a corrupt priesthood: "Take heed that no man deceive you; for many shall come in my name, saying—I am Christ—and shall deceive many; Then shall they deliver you up to be afflicted, and shall kill you, and ye shall be hated of all nations, for my name's sake" (Joseph Smith—Matthew 1:5–7). Surely the message was sobering: You will be hated of all nations, and they will both afflict you and kill you. But who in those nations were the disciples being warned against? According to what we have just read, it was false Christs. Two important implications here are, first, the Twelve would be betrayed by professing Christians, not by those in the world, as we have so often been told; and second, the betraying of the faith would spread to all the world. It didn't matter where the Twelve went; they would be opposed and betrayed. That conclusion is sustained by Nephi in his prophetic dream: "Behold the world and the wisdom thereof: yea, behold the house of Israel hath gathered together to fight against the twelve apostles of the Lamb" (1 Nephi 11:35). The Book of Mormon confirms that it was a love of the world, its traditions, and its sophistry, that caused the house of Israel to betray the apostles and their testimony.

We can reconstruct the story only in part, but that is sufficient to establish a pattern. The apostles took the message to the various nations. Many were converted but not in full. The Christian convert stood alone, overshadowed by the influence of the Jewish temple on the one hand and the Greek academy on the other. From the temple came the Judaizers, who wouldn't let go of their traditions; while from the academy came those indoctrinated in the monotheism of Plato. As if that were not enough, there were also the Gnostics, who were truer than true, straining everything through the veil of mysticism. And so the newly converted, wanting neither to give offense nor to appear as fools, sought common ground and a spirit of conciliation. In so doing, they modified the Christian message until it passed as it were into a new dialect, one that would have been very strange to the ear of those initially commissioned by Christ.[4]

The God of scripture, the God of the prophets, the God testified of by Christ, is not the God of Christian creeds. When Jesus said to Philip, "He that hath seen me hath seen the Father" (John 14:9), he did not have in mind a bodiless, partless, passionless essence with a center everywhere and a circumference nowhere. When he told the Twelve that "my Father is greater than I" (John 14:28), he did not have in mind the idea that he and his Father were of the same essence. In his great intercessory prayer, when he said, "This is life eternal, that they might know thee the only true God, and Jesus Christ, whom thou hast sent" (John 17:3), he did not have in mind the notion that God is an incomprehensible mystery. When he prayed, "Abba, Father [meaning Papa, Papa], take this cup from me" (Mark 14:36), he was not praying to another part of his own essence, nor was he doing so when he pleaded on the cross, "My God, my God, why hast thou forsaken me?" (Matthew 27:46). And when he on that first Easter morning said to Mary, "I ascend unto my Father, and your Father; and to my God, and your God" (John 20:17), he was not suggesting that we are only the children of God in some vague and metaphorical sense.

THE RESTORATION OF DIVINE TRUTHS

Historical and scriptural evidence affirms that the Saints at the time of Christ believed in a God who was a personal being, one who was both corporeal and anthropomorphic. This God of whom the scriptures speak spoke face to face with the prophet called to stand at the head of each major gospel dispensation. Adam, scripture attests, walked and talked with God in Eden. Enoch testified that having ascended Mount Simeon, he was clothed with glory and "saw the Lord; and he stood before my face, and he talked with me, even as a man talketh one with another, face to face" (Moses 7:3–4). Noah, we are told, "was a just man, and perfect in his generation; and he walked with God" (Moses 8:27). In the Abraham papyri we read, "Thus I, Abraham, talked with the Lord, face to face, as one man talketh with another; and he told me of the works which his hands had made; and he said unto me: My son, my son (and his hand was stretched out), behold I will show you all these. And he put his hand upon mine eyes, and I saw those things which his hands had made, which were many; and they multiplied before mine eyes, and I could not see the end thereof" (Abraham 3:11–12). As for Moses, the book that bears his name begins: "The words of God, which he spake unto Moses at a time when Moses was caught up into an exceedingly high mountain, and he saw God face to face, and he talked with him, and the glory of God was upon Moses; therefore Moses could endure his presence" (Moses 1:1–2). Peter, who succeeded Christ as the head of the dispensation of the meridian of time, testified, "For we have not followed cunningly devised fables, when we made known unto you the power and coming of our Lord Jesus Christ, but were eyewitnesses of his majesty. For he received from God the Father honour and glory, when there came such a voice to him from the excellent glory, This is my beloved Son, in whom I am well pleased. And this voice which came from heaven we heard, when we were with him in the holy mount. We have also a more sure word of prophecy; whereunto ye do well that ye take heed, as unto a light that shineth in a dark place, until the day dawn, and the day star arise in your hearts" (2 Peter 1:16–19).

From such testimony we conclude that the God of the ancients was a personal being who thought it not beneath his dignity to appear to his prophets and instruct them face to face. He had body, parts, and passions. He had gender, speech, and family, of which he claimed us to be a part. In textual restorations given us through the Prophet Joseph Smith, we learn that God is an exalted, glorified, resurrected man. We are told that we are his children, created in the image and likeness of his body (Moses 6:9). We neither quibble nor hedge the words of the psalmist, who said: "Ye are gods; and all of you are children of the most High" (Psalm 82:6). We accept Christ's affirmation of the literal rendering of those words (John 10:34–36). Our revelations declare Adam to be the "firstborn" of the Father into this earthly sphere (Abraham 1:3; Moses 6:22) and affirm that Christ was the first of his children born in our spirit or premortal state (D&C 93:21). In the pure and undefiled language of Adam, God was known as Man of Holiness and Jesus Christ, his Only Begotten Son (meaning his only son begotten of a mortal woman), is known as Son of Man or Son of Man of Holiness (Moses 6:57). We believe that Mary was the literal mother of Jesus Christ in the flesh and that God was his father. In testifying of Christ, we do not use language in a deceptive or metaphorical sense. Our scripture declares Christ to be the

Son of God "after the manner of the flesh" (1 Nephi 11:18). President Ezra Taft Benson explained: "The Church of Jesus Christ of Latter-day Saints proclaims that Jesus Christ is the Son of God in the most literal sense. The body in which He performed His mission in the flesh was sired by that same Holy Being we worship as God, our Eternal Father. Jesus was not the son of Joseph nor was He begotten by the Holy Ghost. He is the Son of the Eternal Father!"[5] We claim ourselves competent witnesses of the reality of his resurrection and of his divine Sonship. In bearing such a testimony we stand alone, for historical Christianity has branded us heretical.

WE BELIEVE IN THE GRACE OF CHRIST

As Latter-day Saints we believe in Christ. We believe in salvation by his grace. In so saying, our belief in the doctrine of grace expands far beyond that of our sectarian friends. Only in and through him can we be reconciled with God. As we were without the power to create ourselves, so we are without the power to resurrect ourselves. Nor do we have the power to remit our own sins. Our spirits tainted with sin, having no way to cleanse themselves of its effects, would be (save it were for Christ) subject to the author of sin. We would be citizens of his kingdom. Lucifer would be our king, and we would have to worship him because there would be neither freedom nor agency. Indeed, there would be no light or truth, for Christ is the author of both. In testifying of the grace of Christ, we have in mind more than the idea that he cleanses us from sin. He frees us from the dominion and power of the adversary. He makes possible the inseparable union of our body and spirit that we might experience a fulness of joy, which embraces our becoming heirs of God and joint heirs with Christ, having claim on the fulness of the Father. Through his grace we can become equal with God in power, might, and dominion. Thus Christ's atonement frees us not only from spiritual death (the separation from the presence of God) but from physical death (the separation of our spirit from our physical body). Exaltation consists of our having an exalted, resurrected, and glorified body. It consists in the continuation of the love between a man and his wife, between parents and their children throughout endless generations.

No such blessings or promises are known in the sectarian world. Only Mormonism holds the hope of our obtaining perfected corporeal bodies in the resurrection. Only Mormonism contains the doctrine of eternal marriage and the continuation of the family unit as a tenet of belief. We claim such blessings only in and through the grace of Christ.

WHY WE BELIEVE IN CHRIST

We believe in Christ because we know him. We are his special witnesses in this dispensation. Our tradition does not embrace the idea that the canon of scripture is complete or that the heavens are sealed or that God is some abstract mystery. We will take the testimony of Christ as it is found in the Book of Mormon to those of every nation, kindred, and tongue. We will tell the story of the First Vision describing the appearance of both the Father and the Son. We will build temples among all peoples in order that "the Son of Man might have a place to manifest himself to his people" (D&C 109:5). We will continue to sustain living prophets, seers, and revelators. We possess the Spirit of revelation, and we accept the promise that he will make himself known to us. By revelation he has said: "It shall come to pass that every soul who forsaketh his sins and cometh unto me, and calleth on my name, and obeyeth my voice, and keepeth my commandments, shall see my face and know that I am" (D&C 93:1). The very purpose for which the priesthood was restored was so that the heavens might be opened and that we might commune with the general assembly and church of the Firstborn and "enjoy the communion and presence of God the Father, and Jesus the mediator of the new covenant" (D&C 107:19).

We believe in Christ because of our own experiences and association with him. All accountable persons are invited to the waters of baptism; all are to have hands laid upon their heads and receive the promise of the companionship of the Holy Ghost. All are invited to the house of the Lord to be endowed with power from on high, and all are entitled to a perfect knowledge of both the Father and the Son.

BELIEF IN CHRIST IS A CALL TO DISCIPLESHIP

We accept the witness of Christ, which is ours as a call to discipleship. This we understand to be more than the invitation to learn of him. It involves an obligation of discipline and obedience. The principles taught by the Master must find application in the life of the true disciple. In the New Testament, discipleship was not confined to the Twelve but rather included all true believers. All these enjoyed his love and sought in that spirit to share their knowledge and testimony with others. They sought to imitate the Master. They sought neither to add to nor take from his teachings but rather to follow him. They understood that by sharing his gospel with others they would draw closer to him. Theirs was a close and intimate relationship involving the following seven principles.

To believe in Christ is to believe the doctrines of Christ. Many profess a belief in Christ, but it is a belief without the discipline of true discipleship. James would call it faith without works (see James 2:14). Often it is a belief devoid of any serious doctrinal commitment. As long as it can be maintained that God is an incomprehensible mystery, it can also be maintained that what we believe is of no particular importance. Once the God of heaven manifests himself, then knowledge becomes sure and mankind immediately becomes accountable to follow his path.

To believe in Christ is to accept those who come in his name. The angel of the Lord instructed Adam and Eve that they were to do all that they did "in the name of the Son" and that they should "repent and call upon God in the name of the Son forevermore" (Moses 5:8). In the concept of a name we find both power and authority. Thus we find the expression, "Blessed be the name of God" in Adam's testimony (Moses 5:10), King Benjamin exhorting his people to exercise "faith on his name" (Mosiah 3:9, 21), Alma promising that "he shall bring salvation to all those who shall believe on his name" (Alma 34:15), and the Lord instructing Joseph Smith "that all men must repent and believe on the name of Jesus Christ, and worship the Father in his name, and endure in faith on his name to the end, or they cannot be saved in the kingdom of God" (D&C 20:29). The emphasis in such expressions centers on the name of Christ rather than on the person of Christ. No slight to the person of Christ is intended, but rather the emphasis is on the authority of Christ as it is manifest in such as Adam, King Benjamin, Alma, and Joseph Smith, for in such is found the authority to teach his doctrine and perform the ordinances of salvation.

"Whosoever receiveth my word receiveth me," the Savior said, and "whosoever receiveth me, receiveth those, the First Presidency, whom I have sent, whom I have made counselors for my name's sake unto you" (D&C 112:20). To the meridian Twelve the Lord said, "He that receiveth you receiveth me, and he that receiveth me receiveth him that sent me. He that receiveth a prophet in the name of a prophet shall receive a prophet's reward; and he that receiveth a righteous man in the name of a righteous man shall receive a righteous man's reward" (Matthew 10:40–41). This principle finds expression in what we know as the oath and covenant of the Melchizedek Priesthood.

"All they who receive this priesthood receive me," the Lord said, "for he that receiveth my servants receiveth me; and he that receiveth me receiveth my Father; and he that receiveth my Father receiveth my Father's kingdom; therefore all that my Father hath shall be given unto him" (D&C 84:35–38).

Clearly the message in these and many similar passages of scripture is that it is not enough for us to profess an acceptance of Christ to have claim to salvation. We must also accept those whom he has sent in his name.

To believe in Christ is to live the doctrines of Christ and endure in faith to the end. The true disciple cannot say to God, "I will be your disciple but without chastity," or "I will consecrate myself but leave my wealth intact," or "I will follow you but not your prophet," or "I will be your servant, but I will not comply with the ordinances of salvation."

Responsibility attends true discipleship. Such discipleship must recognize Jesus as Lord and Master. It is with bowed knee that we have been invited to present to the Lord the full measure of our "heart, might, mind and strength" that we might "stand blameless before God at the last day" (D&C 4:2).

A young man told me once that his uncle, who was not a member of the Church, was the most Christian man he had ever known. To illustrate his point he told me about some of the kind and generous things this man had done for others. I enthusiastically agreed that his uncle was a generous man but I could not agree that he was a Christlike man. I asked him if his uncle had been baptized. He said no. I asked if Christ was baptized. He said yes. I asked if his uncle kept the Sabbath holy. He said no. I asked if Christ kept the Sabbath holy. He said yes. I asked if his uncle was a man of prayer. He said no. I asked if Christ was a man of prayer. He said yes. I asked if he remembered Abinadi's description of Christ as one whose will was swallowed up in that of his Father (Mosiah 15:7). He said yes. I asked if he could say that his uncle's life was consumed with doing the will of God. He said no. I asked if the bishop or home teachers invited his uncle to church, would he come? He said that his uncle had been invited to church countless times but that he would not come. I told him that I didn't think his uncle resembled Christ very much, though I knew a lot of members of the Church who did.

To believe in Christ is to accept the reality of the remission of our sins. Stephen Robinson observes: "Unfortunately, there are many members of the Church who simply do not believe this. Though they claim to have testimonies of Christ and of his gospel, they reject the witness of the scriptures and of the prophets about the good news of Christ's atonement. Often these people naively hold on to mutually contradictory propositions without even realizing the nature of the contradiction. For example, they may believe that the Church is true, that Jesus is the Christ, and that Joseph Smith was a prophet of God, while at the same time refusing to accept the possibility of their own complete forgiveness and eventual exaltation in the kingdom of God. They believe *in* Christ, but they do not *believe* Christ. He says, 'Though your sins be as scarlet, they shall be as white as snow. I can make you pure and worthy and celestial,' and they answer back, 'No, you can't. The gospel only works for other people; it won't work for me.'"[6]

To believe in Christ is to trust the verity of his word. It is to believe that he "cannot look upon sin with the least degree of allowance" and that "he that repents and does the commandments of the Lord shall be forgiven" (D&C 1:31–32).

To believe in Christ is to constantly grow in the knowledge and testimony of Christ. "He that doeth truth," wrote John the Beloved, "cometh to the light, that his deeds may be made manifest, that they are wrought in God" (John 3:21). Singularly, John describes "truth" as something we "do" rather than something we are expected to "believe." To those who thought they could divorce belief from action, John said that to say we have fellowship with God while we are walking in the dark "we lie, and do not the truth" (1 John 1:6). His doctrines, Christ said, were not his but the Father's, who sent him. "If any man will do his will, he shall know of the doctrine, whether it be of God, or whether I speak of myself" (John 7:16–17). The Christ of whom we bear witness advanced from grace to grace in the realm of spiritual things until he received the fulness of his Father. Those who truly worship him will be found doing likewise.

To believe in Christ is to seek to share the gospel with others. Inherent in membership in the family of true believers is the responsibility of sharing the message of salvation with others. As we have noted previously, no church could seriously claim to be the rightful steward of the message of salvation without at the same time assuming the obligation of taking that message to every nation, kindred, and tongue. The message of salvation must be available to all and the terms of salvation everlastingly the same. Those terms as declared anew in this dispensation are faith in Christ and his divine Sonship, repentance of sin, baptism by immersion by one having authority, obtaining the gift of the Holy Ghost by the laying on of hands, and enduring in faith to the end.

The responsibility of declaring the gospel rests primarily with those who hold the Melchizedek Priesthood. Those "embracing this calling," the Lord said, "shall be ordained and sent forth to preach the everlasting gospel among the nations—crying repentance, saying: Save yourselves from this untoward generation, and come forth out of the fire, hating even the garments spotted with the flesh. And this commandment shall be given unto the elders of my church, that every man which will embrace it with singleness of heart may be ordained and sent forth, even as I have spoken" (D&C 36:5–7).

To believe in Christ is to bring forth works of righteousness contin-uously. Having placed ourselves on the path that leads to the man-sions of the Father, we "must press forward with a steadfastness in Christ, having a perfect brightness of hope, and a love of God and of all men. Wherefore, if ye shall press forward, feasting upon the word of Christ, and endure to the end, behold, thus saith the Father: Ye shall have eternal life" (2 Nephi 31:20–21). This, we are told, is the way, for there is none other way nor name whereby mankind can be saved. Elder Bruce R. McConkie stated: "Everyone in the Church who is on the straight and narrow path, who is striving and strug-gling and desiring to do what is right, though is far from perfect in this life; if he passes out of this life while he's on the straight and narrow, he's going to go on to eternal reward in his Father's king-dom.

"We don't need to get a complex or get a feeling that you have to be perfect to be saved. You don't. There's only been one perfect person, and that's the Lord Jesus, but in order to be saved in the Kingdom of God and in order to pass the test of mortality, what you have to do is get on the straight and narrow path—thus charting a course leading to eternal life—and then, being on that path, pass out of this life in full fellowship. I'm not saying that you don't have to keep the commandments. I'm saying you don't have to be perfect to be saved. If you did, no one would be saved. The way it operates is this: You get on the path that's named the 'straight and narrow.' You do it by entering at the gate of repentance and baptism. The straight and narrow path leads from the gate of repentance and baptism, a very great distance, to a reward that is called eternal life. If you're on that path and pressing forward, and you die, you'll never get off the path. There is no such thing as falling off the straight and narrow path in the life to come, and the reason is that this life is the time that is given to men to prepare for eternity. Now is the time and the day of your salvation, so if you're working zealously in this life—

though you haven't fully overcome the world and you haven't done all you hoped you might do—you're still going to be saved. You don't have to do what Jacob said, 'Go beyond the mark.' You don't have to live a life that's truer than true. You don't have to have an excessive zeal that becomes fanatical and becomes unbalancing. What you have to do is stay in the mainstream of the Church and live as upright and decent people live in the Church—keeping the commandments, paying your tithing, serving in the organizations of the Church, loving the Lord, staying on the straight and narrow path. If you're on that path when death comes—because this is the time and the day appointed, this the probationary estate—you'll never fall from it, and, for all practical purposes, your calling and election is made sure. Now, that isn't the definition of that term, but the end result will be the same."[7]

"By their fruits ye shall know them," the Savior said (Matthew 7:20). If a tree ceases to bring forth good fruits, we would know it no longer as a good tree. The true believer in Christ does not long for some future time when he can cease praying, quit keeping his covenants, and depart from the straight and narrow path. To believe in Christ is to be constant in works of righteousness.

To believe in Christ is to experience the signs that follow them that believe. Joseph Smith stated: "When faith comes it brings its train of attendants with it—apostles, prophets, evangelists, pastors, teachers, gifts, wisdom, knowledge, miracles, healings, tongues, interpretation of tongues, etc. All these appear when faith appears on the earth; . . . for these are the effects of faith, and always have attended, and always will, attend it. For where faith is, there will the knowledge of God be also, with all things which pertain thereto—revelations, visions, and dreams, as well as every necessary thing, in order that the possessors of faith may be perfected, and obtain salvation."[8] To those holding the priesthood restored to Joseph Smith and Oliver

Cowdery by Peter, James, and John, the Lord said: "As I said unto mine apostles I say unto you again, that every soul who believeth on your words, and is baptized by water for the remission of sins, shall receive the Holy Ghost. And these signs shall follow them that believe—in my name they shall do many wonderful works; in my name they shall cast out devils; in my name they shall heal the sick; in my name they shall open the eyes of the blind, and unstop the ears of the deaf; and the tongue of the dumb shall speak; and if any man shall administer poison unto them it shall not hurt them; and the poison of a serpent shall not have power to harm them" (D&C 84:64–72).

JOSEPH SMITH'S TESTIMONY OF CHRIST

From the First Vision in the spring of 1820, when Joseph Smith was told by Christ that he should join none of the churches of the day because they were "all wrong," their "creeds were an abomination," and their professors "all corrupt," until his tragic death in June 1844, Joseph Smith was prepared to stand alone in the testimony that he bore (Joseph Smith–History 1:19). On one occasion he said: "The object with me is to obey and teach others to obey God in just what He tells us to do. It mattereth not whether the principle is popular or unpopular, I will always maintain a true principle, even if I stand alone in it."[9]

Joseph Smith made no attempt to reconcile what he taught with popularly held tenets of the day. Relative to his testimony of Christ he stood distinctively alone. He boldly set forth his position: "The great designs of God in relation to the salvation of the human family, are very little understood by the professedly wise and intelligent generation in which we live."[10] In the preface to the Doctrine and Covenants, Joseph Smith recorded: "They [referring to those who fail to heed the ordained servants of the Lord] seek not the Lord to establish his righteousness, but every man walketh in his own way, and after the image of his own god, whose image is in the likeness of the world, and whose substance is that of an idol, which waxeth old and shall perish in Babylon, even Babylon the great, which shall fall" (D&C 1:16).

Joseph Smith was a competent witness. His testimony was not based on philosophical speculation but rather on revelation. He read the injunction of James to ask of God, and he did so. Having had the heavens opened to them, Joseph Smith and Sidney Rigdon penned this testimony: "We beheld the glory of the Son, on the right hand of the Father, and received of his fulness; and saw the holy angels, and them who are sanctified before his throne, worshiping God, and the Lamb, who worship him forever and ever. And now, after the many testimonies which have been given of him, this is the testimony, last of all, which we give of him: That he lives! For we saw him, even on the right hand of God; and we heard the voice bearing record that he is the Only Begotten of the Father—That by him, and through him, and of him, the worlds are and were created, and the inhabitants thereof are begotten sons and daughters unto God" (D&C 76:20–24).

Joseph Smith drank at the fountainhead. On one occasion he said, "Could you gaze into heaven five minutes, you would know more than you would by reading all that ever was written on the subject."[11] On another occasion he said, "One truth revealed from heaven is worth all the sectarian notions in existence."[12]

Of his testimony of God, the Prophet said, "I defy all the learning and wisdom and all the combined powers of earth and hell together to refute it."[13] On another occasion he taught, "If any revelations are given of God, they are universally opposed by the priests and Christendom at large; for they reveal their wickedness and abominations."[14] In one of his sermons about God, Joseph Smith said, "The sectarian priests are blind, and they lead the blind, and they will all fall into the ditch together."[15] As to the source of his knowledge, Joseph Smith asked, "Did I build on any other man's foundation? I have got all the truth which the Christian world possessed, and an independent revelation in the bargain, and God will bear me off triumphant."[16]

Such is the doctrine and spirit of the Latter-day Saint testimony of Christ. The first paper published by the Church was the *Evening and Morning Star.* One of its first issues set forth the Latter-day Saint source for finding truth: "Search the Scriptures—*search the revelations which we publish,* and ask your Heavenly Father, in the name of His Son Jesus Christ, to manifest the truth unto you, and if you do it with an eye single to His glory, nothing doubting, He will answer you by the power of His Holy Spirit. You will then know for yourselves and not for another. You will not then be dependent on man for the knowledge of God; nor will there be any room for speculation."[17]

NOTES

1. Will Durant, *Caesar and Christ,* vol. 3 of The Story of Civilization (New York: Simon and Schuster, 1944), p. 660.

2. *The Cambridge History of the Bible,* ed. P. R. Ackroyd and C. F. Evans, 3 vols. (Cambridge: Cambridge University Press, 1970), 1:452.

3. *The Oxford Dictionary of the Christian Church,* ed. F. L. Cross (Oxford: Oxford University Press, 1990), p. 576.

4. See Joseph Fielding McConkie, "False Christs," in *Watch and Be Ready: Preparing for the Second Coming of the Lord* (Salt Lake City: Deseret Book, 1994), pp. 41–42.

5. Ezra Taft Benson, *Come unto Christ* (Salt Lake City: Deseret Book, 1983), p. 4.

6. Stephen E. Robinson, *Believing Christ* (Salt Lake City: Deseret Book, 1992), pp. 8–9.

7. Bruce R. McConkie, *The Probationary Test of Mortality,* address delivered at Institute of Religion, Salt Lake City, Utah, 10 Jan. 1982.

8. Joseph Smith, *Lectures on Faith* (Salt Lake City: Deseret Book, 1985), 7:20, p. 83.

9. Joseph Smith, *History of The Church of Jesus Christ of Latter-day Saints,* 7 vols., 2d ed. rev., ed. B. H. Roberts (Salt Lake City: The Church of Jesus Christ of Latter-day Saints, 1932–51), 6:223.

10. Smith, *History of the Church,* 4:595.

11. Smith, *History of the Church,* 6:50.

12. Smith, *History of the Church,* 6:252.

13. Smith, *History of the Church,* 6:306.

14. Smith, *History of the Church,* 4:588.

15. Smith, *History of the Church,* 5:426.

16. Smith, *History of the Church,* 6:479.

17. *Evening and Morning Star* 1 (July 1832): 22; emphasis added).

Chapter Ten

HERE WE STAND

There is not a man or woman that loves the truth, who has heard the report of the Book of Mormon, but the Spirit of the Almighty has testified to him or her of its truth; neither has any man heard the name of Joseph Smith, but the Spirit has whispered to him—"He is a true Prophet."
—Brigham Young

THERE IS A SPIRIT AND A POWER we enjoy when we are true to the message the Lord has given us that can be experienced in no other way. Surely the Spirit is anxious to bear witness to the truths we have been commissioned to declare. We can go out under the guise of telling the world about family home evening, but Christ did not shed his blood on Calvary, nor Joseph and Hyrum Smith theirs in Carthage, so that we might take the family home evening manual to those of every nation, kindred, tongue, and people. As wonderful as that program is, it is powerless to remit sins or seal families for time and eternity. The message we have been given to deliver has the power of God in it, and no one worthy of the company of the Spirit can declare that message without enjoying that companionship.

OUR OWN GROUND

For generations it has been the practice to seek to give the gospel message respectability by sustaining it with proof texts from the Bible. When I went into the mission field more than thirty years ago, we were all armed with our pocket edition of *Ready References* to which we could turn to find biblical support for all Mormon doctrines. Upon our arrival in the mission field, we were handed a long list of scriptures and told to memorize a passage every day. We conscientiously tried to do so. Virtually all of those passages came from the Bible. Our reading assignments consisted of the standard works and books that reinforced the idea that all we do and believe can be justified by the Bible. Quoting from the Doctrine and Covenants in a cottage meeting was unheard of.

I remember a cottage meeting in which a man we were teaching asked about John 4:24, which says, "God is a spirit." My senior companion, who was then an assistant to the mission president, said, "Yes, it is true that the scriptures say 'God is a spirit,' but they also say 'Man is spirit.'" That, of course, is true, but the second text is found in Doctrine and Covenants 93:33, not in the Bible. Because the room was crowded, my companion was sitting slightly in front of me. As he gave his answer he put his hand behind his back, where only I could see it, and crossed his fingers. We were both greatly relieved that no one asked for the source of his text. After we left that home, my companion put his arm around my shoulder and said, "Well, we really got away with one in there, didn't we!" We felt like a couple of schoolboys who had cheated on an exam without getting caught.

The story is a sad one. Neither my companion nor I understood the message that we had been commissioned to teach. How ironic that we thought we had "cheated" by quoting one of the revelations of the Restoration, when in truth those revelations were the very reason the Lord had sent us out as missionaries! Our whole message centers on the reality of living prophets, modern revelation, and authority restored anew from the heavens. If we had truly understood the reason the Lord had sent us, we could have responded, "Certainly, it is true that God is a spirit, even as man is a spirit. But through a revelation given to a prophet in our day, we know that God is a personal being, a loving Father who has body, parts, and passions. When the scriptures say we are in his image and likeness, they mean it in a very literal sense." The Holy Ghost would have sustained us in making such a declaration, and it would have opened the door to a meaningful gospel discussion. Perhaps the fact that those people, like so many others we attempted to teach, did not continue with the discussions and did not join the Church had something to do with our failure to be true to the message the Lord had given us. That we had learned to rely on Bible texts may not only have made it more difficult for our investigators to understand but also more difficult for the Spirit to witness to its truthfulness.

The need to understand the necessity to be true to our message is not confined to missionaries alone. A woman called our home one evening to tell me that she was having a discussion with a non-member neighbor—not an argument—and what she needed, she said, was a scriptural reference to prove that God has a body. I directed her to Doctrine and Covenants 130:22, which reads: "The Father has a body of flesh and bones as tangible as man's; the Son also; but the Holy Ghost has not a body of flesh and bones, but is a personage of Spirit. Were it not so, the Holy Ghost could not dwell in us." Surely that is as plain and to the point as language permits.

My caller immediately objected. "What I need," she said, "is a Bible passage."

Now, I happen to know that there are more than five hundred

passages of scriptures in the Bible that can be used to argue that God has a body, but I also know that such an argument is fruitless. We read our Bible text and say, "See, there's the proof." But no one ever responds by saying, "Wow, I didn't know that! May I be baptized?" What they say is, "The scriptures you are reading were not intended to be understood literally. They are simply figurative representations of God. If you are going to accept everything in the Bible as being literal, then when it says God is 'the rock of our salvation' you must believe he is a rock; or when it says he will keep us under the shadow of his wings, you must believe God is a bird and has wings." The discussion gets silly very quickly, and the silliest thing about it is that we allow ourselves to be a part of it.

So I told my caller that the way we knew that God had a body was that he told us and that we had no better authority than that. We hadn't learned it from the Bible. With a tone of disappointment in her voice she said, "Well, thanks, anyway. I'll see if I can find someone else who can help me," and hung up.

I have been through that kind of experience again and again. A young man came to my office one morning before class and told me that he just about had his nonmember roommate converted. "All I need," he said, "is a passage of scripture that proves that marriages are supposed to be eternal. Can you help me?" he asked.

"That's easy enough," I said. "We have God's word on the matter in Doctrine and Covenants 132."

"No, no," he interjected, "what I need is a Bible passage."

"We are not practicing eternal marriage because of any Bible text," I responded. "We do it because God commanded us to do so through a living prophet."

"You mean you don't know of any Bible text that proves it?" he asked, tension and anxiety ringing in his voice.

"I don't even know a Bible text that I can torture into saying such a thing," I replied.

He responded, "I'd better see if there isn't someone else who can help me," and left abruptly.

The perspective represented by these exchanges, which is not an uncommon one, is a matter of considerable concern. It ignores the fact that there has been a restoration of the gospel. It represents a retreat to the Protestant position that the Bible is the final word on all things. It makes us a part of the argument over the meaning of the Bible instead of the solution to that argument. It is a way of saying that dead prophets outrank living ones and that modern revelation can be accepted only if Bible texts prove it to be true. This perspective short-circuits the conversion process and effectually denies the reality of the First Vision. It turns a deaf ear to every revelation we have received since the spring of 1820.

We know by experience that it is easier to convert people to the Book of Mormon than it is to convince them that we are interpreting the Bible correctly. We also know that conversion will unlock for them the true spirit and power of the Bible. Our efforts to convert people by using Bible texts may have no other effect than sustaining the notion that the Bible, rather than the voice of God in our dispensation, is the source of salvation. If that is the case, there would have been no need for a restoration of the gospel. All of the prophetic messengers who came with keys, powers, and authorities would have come in vain.

The Book of Mormon testifies that many of the plain and precious parts of the Bible were taken from it before it went forth to the nations of the earth (see 1 Nephi 13:23–29). We can hardly be true to the book if we argue that all its doctrines can be found in the Bible. Such arguments remind me of the occasion when a very enterprising student came into my office carrying a manuscript of impressive proportions. He placed it on my desk and said he was anxious to take it to a publisher but wanted me to review it for him first. He explained that it was a defense of Mormonism in which he had proved all our doctrines by the Bible. I asked him to close the door and in hushed tones said, "We have to get rid of this as quickly as we can!" There was obvious alarm in his voice when he asked what I meant. I said, "Look, if you have proven all of our doctrines by the Bible, then there is no need for Joseph Smith and the revelations of the Restoration." I added, with some emphasis, "This thing could destroy everything we stand for!" He grabbed his manuscript and made a quick exit.

DO MORMONS WORSHIP JOSEPH SMITH?

Our commission is to bear witness of the restored gospel in all the world. Any time the adversary can get us to substitute something else for that message, the victory is his. It is not our purpose to convert people to programs, to activities, or to a Latter-day Saint culture. Nor can we modify the message the Lord gave us in an attempt to be more acceptable. To make such things the focus of our efforts is to lose sight of our destiny and purpose and will eventually cause us to lose our own way. To properly present our message requires that we testify that Joseph Smith is the great prophet of the Restoration. There is power in such a testimony, and every effort is made by the adversary to keep us from bearing it. Perhaps his most effective ploy is the notion that we should not testify about Joseph Smith for fear that people will think we worship him instead of Christ. The idea is to emphasize our faith in Christ while avoiding reference to Joseph Smith.

We hope that such an approach will place us in a position to say to those of other Christian faiths, "We share your love and reverence for Christ." But if we succeed in convincing our friends of other faiths that we share their reverence for and testimony of Christ, we have left them no reason to join with us. Such a ploy is self-defeating. And perhaps the greater danger is that we may convince ourselves, or even our children, that we *do* have the same faith. We then become embarrassed by the idea that there is one true church and adopt a Protestant idea that there is no greater difference between our faith and those of the world than there is between Methodists and Presbyterians.

The desire for acceptance can make setting aside both the essence of our faith and our religious heritage a relatively simple thing. The Reorganized Church of Jesus Christ of Latter Day Saints has now reinterpreted the First Vision in such a manner that they are comfortable with the following language, which is taken from the dedication service of their new temple in Independence, Missouri:

Let us rejoice

. . . for the courage of St. Ignatius, who was slain
praising Christ's love.

. . . for the martyrdom of Blandina, slave woman, during
the cruel reign of Marcus Aurelius.

. . . for the Monastic tradition, which helped to keep
Christianity alive, and to preserve the scriptural
witness to God's unfailing love.

. . . for the impact of these, and others, on our faith:
Calvin, Luther, the Wesleys, Simon Bolivar,
Dorothea Dix, Joseph and Emma Hale Smith, the
Grimke sisters, Susan B. Anthony, Margaret
Fuller, Sigmund Freud, Marie Curie, Mahatma
Gandhi, and Toyohiko Kagawa.[1]

The prayer is an olive branch extended to those of historical Christianity with whom the RLDS seek fellowship. Such is their prerogative, and we wish them well in doing so. But we as Latter-day Saints cannot assume such a stance. As long as the First Vision stands as the foundation of our faith, we stand alone. We can neither seek nor accept any other companionship or alliance.

Let me illustrate in principle what is involved. Recently my wife and I were invited to speak to a group of seminary students on the subject of preparing for missions. Before we spoke, two of their number, a young woman and a young man, were asked to bear a brief testimony, apparently without warning. Obviously, the hope in calling on them was to simulate the opportunity they would have as missionaries and to invite the Spirit into our meeting. Neither student handled the situation very appropriately, and the hoped-for end was not accomplished. Because of that, as I began my talk, I suggested to the students that if they were called on, as two of their peers had just been, they could assure themselves and those present of a positive spiritual experience by testifying that Joseph Smith is a prophet. I assured them that if they would do that, the Spirit would quicken their minds and let them know what they should say. After the meeting, one of the teachers asked if he could speak with me privately for a moment. He asked delicately, "Would it not have been more appropriate to tell the students that when called on unexpectedly to speak, they should testify of Christ and then extend the promise of the sustaining support of the Spirit?" He seemed stunned when I answered, "No."

I went on to tell him that the fact that Christ is the foundation of our faith is beyond question, nor can the importance of his role as our Savior or Redeemer be overstated. Every principle of the gospel stems from his atoning sacrifice. We are saved through his grace, and without his saving labors in our behalf there would be no salvation. Such principles cannot be compromised. Why then testify that Joseph Smith is his prophet? Because it is in the Book of Mormon that we find our knowledge and understanding of both the Fall and the Atonement (see 2 Nephi 2; 9); and because it was from the Prophet Joseph Smith that we learned that all principles of the gospel are simply an appendage to the Atonement.[2] We exist as a church because there was a Joseph Smith. It is because there is a Book of Mormon, it is because John the Baptist came to the Prophet and gave him keys and authority, and because Peter, James, and John did likewise. Our testimony of Christ grows out of these truths; it cannot stand independent of them. We cannot bring people to Christ without bringing them to these principles. We testify of Joseph Smith because he is God's choice to be the revelator of Christ for this dispensation. We testify of the truthfulness of the Book of Mormon because it is the pure source, given by God to our dispensation, to learn of his Son. We testify of the appearance of those who held authority anciently to Joseph Smith, because that evidences that God has given us the same knowledge and authority had by the ancients. If we are going to ignore those principles in the testimony we bear, then it is a reasonable assumption that the Spirit will ignore us when we attempt to bear that testimony. "You shall declare the things which have been revealed to my servant, Joseph Smith, Jun.," is the Lord's direction to us (D&C 31:4). The eyes of that young seminary teacher lighted up, and he enthusiastically started telling me how his missionary experiences sustained the principle.

Other missionaries have had similar experiences. Brigham Young used the following story to teach this principle: "One of our Elders with whom I was acquainted, after he was baptised, got cornered up, and was obliged to preach a sermon. He never had been able to say that he knew Joseph was a Prophet; but he was there in the meeting: the house was crowded with the congregation; the windows and doors full of people, and all around on the green waiting to hear a 'Mormon' preacher. There were none there but this one man, and he was called upon to preach. He thought he would pray and dismiss the meeting. He never had known that Joseph Smith was a Prophet: that was the lion that lay in his path; and he could not get by him, nor round about him, nor dig under him, nor leap over him; and the lion he must meet: he must say Joseph, for better or worse. As soon as he got 'Joseph' out, 'is a Prophet' was the next; and from that, his tongue was loosened, and he continued talking until near sundown. The Lord pours out his Spirit upon a man when he testifies that which the Lord gives him to testify of. From that day to this, he has never been at a loss to know that Joseph was a Prophet."[3]

Similarly, Matthew Cowley shared this experience: "I will never forget the prayers of my father the day that I left. I have never heard a more beautiful blessing in all my life. Then his last words to me at the railroad station, 'My boy, you will go out on that mission; you will study; you will try to prepare your sermons; and sometimes when you are called upon, you will think you are wonderfully prepared, but when you stand up, your mind will go completely blank.' I have had that experience more than once.

"I said, 'What do you do when your mind goes blank?'

"He said, 'You stand up there and with all the fervor of your soul, you bear witness that Joseph Smith was a prophet of the living God, and thoughts will flood into your mind and words to your mouth, to round out those thoughts in a facility of expression that will carry conviction to the heart of everyone who listens.' And so my mind, being mostly blank during my five years in the mission field, gave me the opportunity to bear testimony to the greatest event in the history of the world since the crucifixion of the Master. Try it sometime, fellows and girls. If you don't have anything else to say, testify that Joseph Smith was the prophet of God, and the whole history of the Church will flood into your mind."[4]

BEING TRUE TO THE TESTIMONY OF THE RESTORATION

At issue here is the courage and conviction to bear witness to the principles that set us apart from the world and require us to stand on our own ground. Parley P. Pratt records an event in the early history of the Church that aptly illustrates the matter. "While visiting with brother Joseph in Philadelphia, a very large church was opened for him to preach in, and about three thousand people assembled to hear him. Brother Rigdon spoke first, and dwelt on the Gospel, illustrating his doctrine by the Bible. When he was through, brother Joseph arose like a lion about to roar; and being full of the Holy Ghost, spoke in great power, bearing testimony of the visions he had seen, the ministering of angels which he had enjoyed; and how he had found the plates of the Book of Mormon, and translated them by the gift and power of God. He commenced by saying: 'If nobody else had the courage to testify of so glorious a message from Heaven, and of the finding of so glorious a record, he felt to do it in justice to the people, and leave the event with God.'

"The entire congregation were astounded; electrified, as it were, and overwhelmed with the sense of the truth and power by which he spoke, and the wonders which he related. A lasting impression was made; many souls were gathered into the fold. And I bear witness, that he, by his faithful and powerful testimony, cleared his garments of their blood. Multitudes were baptized in Philadelphia and in the regions around; while, at the same time, branches were springing up in Pennsylvania, in Jersey and in various directions."[5]

There is some irony associated with this story. Elder Pratt was the missionary who taught John Taylor. Then came the dark days of the Kirtland apostasy. Of that time Elder B. H. Roberts wrote: "There was a bitter spirit of apostasy rife in Kirtland. A number in the quorum of the Twelve were disaffected toward the Prophet, and the Church seemed on the point of disintegration. Among others, Parley P. Pratt was floundering in the darkness, and coming to Elder Taylor told him of some things wherein he considered the Prophet Joseph in error. To his remarks Elder Taylor replied: 'I am surprised to hear you speak so, Brother Parley. Before you left Canada you bore a strong testimony to Joseph Smith being a Prophet of God, and to the truth of the work he has inaugurated; and you said you knew these things by revelation, and the gift of the Holy Ghost. You gave to me a strict charge to the effect that though you or an angel from heaven was to declare anything else I was not to believe it. Now Brother Parley, it is not man that I am following, but the Lord. The principles you taught me led me to Him, and I now have the same testimony that you then rejoiced in. If the work was true six months ago, it is true today; if Joseph was then a prophet, he is now a prophet.'"[6] Because of that testimony, Elder Pratt went to the Prophet "in tears, and, with a broken heart and contrite spirit" to confess and make things right.[7]

One classic illustration of being true to our testimony that Joseph Smith is a prophet centers on a story that President David O. McKay was fond of telling about a missionary experience of his father, who served in his native Scotland. He was president of the Glasgow District when he received a strong witness of the divinity of the mission of the Prophet Joseph Smith. President McKay said:

"I know that the Lord communicates with his servants. I have not doubted this as a fact since I was a boy and heard the testimony of my father regarding the revelation that came to him of the divinity of the mission of the Prophet Joseph. I feel impressed to relate that circumstance and add his testimony to the one that I am now giving. He accepted a call to a mission in 1881. When he began preaching in his native land, and bore testimony of the restoration of the gospel of Jesus Christ, he noticed that the people turned away from him. They were bitter in their hearts against anything Mormon, and the name of Joseph Smith seemed to arouse antagonism in their hearts. One day he concluded that the best way to reach these people would be to preach just the simple principles, the atonement of the Lord Jesus Christ, the first principles of the gospel, and not bear testimony of the restoration. In a month or so he became oppressed with a gloomy, downcast feeling and he could not enter into the spirit of his work. He did not really know what was the matter; but his mind became obstructed; his spirit became depressed; he was oppressed and hampered; and that feeling of depression continued until it weighed him down with such heaviness that he went to the Lord and said: 'Unless I can get this feeling removed, I shall have to go home. I can't continue my work thus hampered.'

"The discouragement continued for some time after that, when, one morning, before daylight, following a sleepless night, he decided to retire to a cave, near the ocean, where he knew he would be shut off from the world entirely, and there pour out his soul to God and ask why he was oppressed with this feeling, what he had done, and what he could do to throw it off and continue his work. He started out in the dark towards the cave. He became so eager to get to it that he started to run. As he was leaving the town, he was hailed by an officer who wanted to know what was the matter. He gave some non-committal but satisfying reply and was permitted to go on. Something just seemed to drive him; he had to get relief. He entered the cave or sheltered opening, and said: 'Oh, Father, what can I do to have this feeling removed? I must have it lifted or I cannot continue in this work'; and he heard a voice, as distinct as the tone I am now uttering, say: 'Testify that Joseph Smith is a Prophet of God.' Remembering then, what he tacitly had decided six weeks or more before, and becoming overwhelmed with the thought, the whole thing came to him in a realization that he was there for a special mission, and he had not given that special mission the attention which it deserved. Then he cried in his heart, 'Lord, it is enough,' and went out from the cave."[8]

Brigham Young illustrated the power associated with the testimony that Joseph Smith is a prophet when he said: "There is not a man or woman that loves the truth, who has heard the report of the Book of Mormon, but the Spirit of the Almighty has testified to him or her of its truth; neither has any man heard the name of Joseph Smith, but the Spirit has whispered to him—'He is a true Prophet.'"[9]

THE IMPORTANCE OF THE FIRST VISION

Speaking at Carthage Jail, where Joseph and Hyrum Smith were martyred, President Howard W. Hunter said on the one hundred fiftieth anniversary of that event, "Joseph Smith's greatness consists in one thing—the truthfulness of his declaration that he saw the Father and the Son and that he responded to the reality of that divine revelation."[10] The First Vision, explained Elder Bruce R. McConkie, "was the most important event that had taken place in all world history from the day of Christ's ministry to the glorious hour when it occurred."[11] This vision stands as a refutation of the fundamental doctrines of a corrupt Christianity. It destroys the very premises upon which all the creeds of Christendom rest.

Whereas traditional Christianity declares that the heavens are sealed and revelation has ceased, the First Vision shatters that seal and reopens the channel of divine communication between God and men.

Whereas traditional Christianity declares God to be invisible, and therefore unseen throughout the immenseness of eternity, the First Vision evidences that he does in reality manifest himself.

Whereas traditional Christianity declares the Father and Son to be without body, parts, and passions, the theophany witnessed by Joseph Smith introduces both the Father and the Son as corporeal beings, each separate from the other.

Whereas traditional Christianity views the fatherhood of God and the sonship of Christ as purely figurative, in the First Vision Joseph Smith actually heard the voice of God testifying that Jesus the Christ was his Son.

As to the churches of the world, Joseph Smith was instructed that he was to join none of them. He, like the church he would yet organize, was to stand independent of the authority and knowledge of the world. The process of salvation must dissociate itself from error and falsehood. The priesthood and all ordinances and doctrines of salvation must stand unsoiled and independent of the sophistry of men; nothing must be added to or taken from them.

In recounting the events that led him to what we have come to know as the Sacred Grove, the Prophet Joseph Smith tells how he was impressed by the injunction of James for all who sought wisdom to ask of God. His description of that experience is a perfect illustration of how the Spirit of revelation speaks through holy writ. "Never," he said, "did any passage of scripture come with more power to the heart of man than this did at this time to mine. It seemed to enter with great force into every feeling of my heart. I reflected on it again and again, knowing that if any person needed wisdom from God, I did; for how to act I did not know, and unless I could get more wisdom than I then had, I would never know" (Joseph Smith–History 1:12). What has been described here is the Spirit of revelation directing Joseph Smith to inquire of the Lord; that is, a revelation directing him to receive a revelation. The experience could leave us wondering how often revelations have gone unclaimed because of our failure to heed the prompting to ask.

Continuing his description of the events leading to the first vision, Joseph Smith then made what may well be the most important observation ever made relative to the manner in which we teach others the gospel. He said: "For the teachers of religion of the different sects understood the same passages of scripture so differently as to destroy all confidence in settling the question by an appeal to the Bible" (Joseph Smith–History 1:12). Had Joseph Smith sought answers in the Bible, instead of on his knees in a quiet grove, we would still be waiting for the restoration of the gospel promised in the Bible. Similarly, in missionary work, as long as we attempt to show people the path of salvation as stemming from the Bible, we become nothing more than another of the squabbling sects of Christendom. Our responsibility is to teach investigators to pray and to show them how answers come. The well-trained missionary will answer investigators' questions by finding the simplest and most direct route to the Sacred Grove. It is not common ground we seek in giving answers, but holy ground. Those who have a Bible need now to become as those of whom we read in the Bible; that is, they need living prophets and the faith to call down the revelations of heaven upon their own heads.

The gospel cannot be properly taught amid the spirit of contention. That is one of the primary reasons we have been given the Book of Mormon. Nephi explained that by placing the Bible and the Book of Mormon together we would be able to confound false doctrines, lay down contentions, and establish peace (2 Nephi 3:12). The Book of Mormon, and in a more general sense the entire message of the Restoration, constitutes that book of peace. Our response to good people who seek to convert us to their interpretation of the Bible is respectful. We simply say that we could agree with them, except for one thing; and that one thing is that God has spoken in our day and has given us a more perfect and complete answer. We make no claim to seeing the Bible more clearly than they do, save only by the light of modern revelation. We would never seek to have anyone surrender their love for the Bible; we seek only to add to it.

At issue here is the principle of revelation. Virtually all anti-Mormon criticism reduces itself to the critic's refusal to concede the reality of revelation. Such criticism attacks the First Vision, the Book of Mormon, the revelations in the Doctrine and Covenants, and the authority of a restored priesthood. Each of those components is rooted in modern revelation. To allow revelation in any form is to allow the possibility that Joseph Smith was, in fact, a prophet and that Mormonism is true. That would never do. To oppose our message demands opposition to our claim that God continues to speak. The process of conversion requires obtaining a conviction of the truthfulness of the restored gospel by personal experience with the principle of revelation. Everyone is required to do what Joseph Smith did, and that is to receive the personal revelation that the wisdom that brings salvation comes only by the Spirit of revelation, and then each must find his own equivalent of the Sacred Grove and obtain his own answer. Having then obtained an answer they, like Joseph Smith, have acquired a faith and knowledge that stands independent of the wisdom of men. Thus it is that each member of the Church has his own gospel dispensation, in the sense that his knowledge and testimony allow him to stand independent of the wisdom of the world. In that sense, every soul must obtain the knowledge of salvation for himself. It cannot be had only from books or schools, colleges or universities, nor is it simply a matter of having been born in the right neighborhood or a favored nation. All must obtain, and all must do so on the same conditions.

OUR DEBT TO OTHERS

The declaration that we stand independent of the doctrines and philosophies of the world is not intended to suggest that we have not been immeasurably blessed by countless souls not of our faith. The freedom of worship that allows the seed of faith to grow has been purchased with the sacrifice and courage of many noble and good people. Sacred ground has been watered with their blood, and they hold a lasting place of honor in our hearts. Nor do we take lightly the countless others whose lives have blessed ours with their sweat and tears, their inspiration and talent, their ingenuity and genius. We make no claim to a monopoly on goodness, virtue, or even truth. Our sole claim is to those singular truths upon which salvation rests and to the authority to perform those ordinances essential to salvation. As to the countless other things of lasting worth in this world, Joseph Smith teaches us, "If there is anything virtuous, lovely, or of good report or praiseworthy, we seek after these things" (Article of Faith

13). The earth has never known a people more devoted to missionary work than the Latter-day Saints, nor do our labors stop there, for we also seek to bless all who once lived on this earth with the fulness of gospel blessings, through our labors in their behalf in our temples. In our missionary labors we have never asked anyone to surrender any true practice, belief, or wholesome association to join with us. We say to these converts, Hold to those truths with all the tenacity of your soul, and we will add to them.

"THY NAME SHALL BE HAD FOR GOOD AND EVIL"

Three years after the First Vision Moroni first appeared to Joseph Smith to begin preparing him to bring forth the Book of Mormon. Moroni began Joseph's instruction with a unique and remarkable prophecy. He told the now seventeen-year-old boy that his name "should be had for good and evil among all nations, kindreds, and tongues, or that it should be both good and evil spoken of among all people" (Joseph Smith–History 1:33). Of all the prophecies associated with the restoration of the gospel in this dispensation, that is the most remarkable. No other prophecy can match it in depth or breadth. In 1823, Joseph Smith was an unknown, uneducated farm boy living in wilderness conditions. What of the seventeen-year-old boys living today? What are the odds that we could pick one of their number, particularly one whose circumstances were as unpromising as those of Joseph Smith, who would yet be known among all the peoples of the earth? There are few young men in earth's history of whom that could be said.

A more bold and far-reaching prophecy could not have been made, and we make no pretense that it has yet been fulfilled. Yet the work moves forward, and no faithful Latter-day Saint has any difficulty seeing that future day when missionaries will labor among all the peoples of the earth. Our concern here, however, is not in the remarkable nature of the prophecy but in the reason for it. Why is it necessary for Joseph Smith's name to be known among all people? Joseph Smith is the great revelator of Christ for our dispensation. The Bible, the Book of Mormon, and the Doctrine and Covenants all declare that there is but one name under heaven whereby men can be saved and that is the name of the Lord Jesus Christ (see Acts 4:12; Mosiah 3:17; D&C 18:23). Joseph Smith is the greatest teacher of Christ the world has ever known. He has restored more scriptural testimony from the ancient disciples of Christ than any man who ever lived; he received and recorded more revelations relative to Christ and his plan for the salvation of his children than any other man who ever lived; and he revealed more of the mysteries of heaven in his discourses than any man of whom the world has record. He was God's covenant spokesman. Every man on the face of the earth today who has the authority to speak or act in the name of God traces that authority to Joseph Smith.

We cannot take the message of salvation to the ends of the earth independent of our witness of Joseph Smith as the great prophet of the Restoration. We can no more declare the message of the restored gospel without mention of Joseph Smith than we can tell the story of Sinai without reference to Moses. We cannot seek to hide the name of Joseph Smith in efforts to share the gospel, for in so doing we will find an immediate absence of the Spirit. For thousands of years the religious world has spoken reverently of the law of Moses, without anyone supposing that those who exercised faith therein worshiped Moses instead of the God of heaven. Why then the inordinate concern on the part of some to dissociate the name of Joseph Smith from the message of the Restoration lest we be accused of worshiping him?

Of course, there are those who will misunderstand and pervert and distort our message. That too was part of the promise given by Moroni. He said that the name of Joseph Smith was to be had for "good and evil" among those of every nation, kindred, tongue, and people. We know that no truth of salvation will ever go unopposed. All heaven-sent truths are to be attested to by both the sweet and peaceful whisperings of the Spirit and the loud, rancorous, and ugly hollering of the legions of the adversary. No truth that has the power to bless lives will be left undisturbed by the prince of darkness. For us to hide that truth ourselves simply saves him the trouble.

A telestial world is often a very uninhabitable place for celestial principles. Yet the greater the opposition, the greater the strength of those who withstand it. It was Moroni's role to prepare the youthful Joseph Smith for such opposition. Moroni explained to Joseph that the work to which he had been called would "cause the righteous to rejoice and wicked to rage; with the one;" he said, "it shall be had in honour, and with the other in reproach; yet, with these it shall be a terror, because of the great and marvelous work which shall follow the coming forth of this fulness of the gospel."[12]

Moroni gave Joseph Smith a sign by which he might know that the things he was being told were true. The sign had particular reference to the coming forth of the Book of Mormon and to its testimony of Christ going to every nation, kindred, tongue, and people. "This is the sign," he said. "When these things begin to be known, that is, when it is known that the Lord has shown you these things, the workers of iniquity will seek your overthrow. They will circulate falsehoods to destroy your reputation; and also will seek to take your life; but remember this, if you are faithful, and shall hereafter continue to keep the commandments of the Lord, you shall be preserved to bring these things forth; for in due time he will give you a commandment to come and take them. When they are interpreted, the Lord will give the holy priesthood to some, and they shall begin to proclaim this gospel and baptize by water, and after that, they shall have power to give the Holy Ghost by the laying on of their hands. Then will persecution rage more and more; for the iniquities of men shall be revealed, and those who are not built upon the Rock will seek to overthrow the church; but it will increase the more opposed."[13]

Joseph Smith soon learned that Moroni had not overstated either the persuasive power of the message that had been given to him or the opposition that it would engender. In a revelation to Joseph Smith in the darkest point of his life, while he was incarcerated in a dungeon that was a part of the Liberty Jail, the Lord told him: "The ends of the earth shall inquire after thy name, and fools shall have thee in derision, and hell shall rage against thee; while the pure in heart, and the wise, and the noble, and the virtuous, shall seek counsel, and authority, and blessings constantly from under thy hand" (D&C 122:1–2).

If we are to stand where Joseph stood, that is, if we are to hold to the same principles and declare the same doctrines, then we too must be known for both good and evil among those with whom we labor. Our efforts will be held in honor by some and in derision by others, yet we must stand firm. Surely this has been the lot of virtually every missionary who has ever served. When Moroni linked Joseph Smith with his destiny, he linked all who would be faithful to that same testimony to that same destiny.

THE KEYSTONE OF OUR RELIGION

We find the following entry in the *History of the Church* for Sunday, November 28, 1841. "I spent the day in council," said Joseph Smith, "with the Twelve Apostles at the house of President Young, conversing with them upon a variety of subjects." Only one, however, merited mention in his journal. "I told the brethren," he said, "that the Book of Mormon was the most correct of any book on earth, and the keystone of our religion, and a man would get nearer to God by abiding by its precepts, than by any other book."[14]

The Book of Mormon is the keystone in the arch of the restored gospel. A keystone rests at the crown of an arch and locks all the other stones in place. As long as the keystone stands, the arch stands. Should the keystone fall, the arch would also fall. So it is with the Book of Mormon. Resting at the crown of the Restoration, it locks all other doctrines in place. If it stands, the Church stands; if it falls, the Church falls. For instance, the Book of Mormon is the perfect evidence that Joseph Smith is a prophet, that Jesus is the Christ and the Son of God, that resurrection—the inseparable union of body and spirit—is a reality, that God remembers the covenants he made with the fathers, and that Israel will be gathered again to the covenants of salvation and then restored to the glory of David's day. The book is itself a miracle and thus establishes the truth that the God of Israel is a God of miracles.

It was in translating this record that Joseph Smith laid the foundation of his own understanding of the gospel's saving principles. As it was with Joseph Smith, so it is to be with each of us. Almost a year before the Church was organized, the Lord instructed Oliver Cowdery, who had been the Prophet's scribe in translating the book, to trust in its doctrines as he sought instruction from the Lord. "Behold," the Lord said, "I have manifested unto you, by my Spirit in many instances, that the things which you have written are true; wherefore you know that they are true. And if you know that they are true, behold, I give unto you a commandment, that you rely upon the things which are written; for in them are all things written concerning the foundation of my church, my gospel, and my rock. Wherefore, if you shall build up my church, upon the foundation of my gospel and my rock, the gates of hell shall not prevail against you" (D&C 18:2–5).

Only after the Book of Mormon and its doctrines had come forth could the Church be organized. The organization was not to call forth those doctrines; rather, the doctrines were to call forth the organization. Thus in teaching our nonmember friends we do not seek to have them obtain a testimony of the organization of the Church but rather a testimony of the doctrines taught in the Book of Mormon. It is through the Book of Mormon, for instance, that we want them to learn of the necessity of baptism. Thus we have been instructed to flood the earth with copies of the Book of Mormon rather than with copies of a chart that details the organization of the Church. For this reason the many scriptural texts describing the events of the last days center on the gathering of Israel rather than on the organization of the Church. Similarly it was necessary for the priesthood to be restored before the Church could be organized. The organization must always be subordinate to the doctrines and the authority that created it. It is here that we must stand, for the idea that the Bible is a sufficient source upon which to base the organization of the Church denies the need for continuous revelation, the need for the restoration of the priesthood, and the need for living oracles. It is to deny that power by which Israel is to be gathered and the host of testimonies from prophets of ages past of a restoration of all things. It is to deny the need for this, the greatest of all gospel dispensations, the one in which all the keys, powers, majesties, glory, and strength of past dispensations are to be gathered to prepare the way for the coming of the Lord.

WHERE WE STAND

As Latter-day Saints we must know clearly where we stand. If our message is simply a reworking of key Bible texts for which we have gained some insights that others overlooked, then why not abandon the offensive notion that there was a universal apostasy, or that there is but one true church, and get on with the matter of mending fences with historical Christianity? If, on the other hand, we are serious in testifying that there was indeed an apostasy, that it was universal, that it included the loss of the priesthood and the saving truths of salvation and the knowledge of the very nature of God himself, then we must be prepared to stand alone. We are not attempting to rebuild out of the theological rubble of the past. We have no borrowed doctrines. We have no priesthood, no keys, no power, no authority that we have received from the world. Such being the case, we have no right to proclaim our message to the nations of the earth by seeking common ground. We must stand independent. Indeed, it is not common ground that we seek. We seek sacred ground, and upon that ground we must stand.

NOTES

1. "Dedication of the Temple," Independence, Missouri, 17 Apr. 1994. Copy of the program in possession of the author.

2. Joseph Smith, *Teachings of the Prophet Joseph Smith,* sel. Joseph Fielding Smith (Salt Lake City: Deseret Book, 1974), p. 121.

3. Brigham Young, in *Journal of Discourses,* 26 vols. (London: Latter-day Saints' Book Depot, 1854–86), 6:280.

4. Matthew Cowley, *Matthew Cowley Speaks* (Salt Lake City: Deseret Book, 1971), pp. 297–98.

5. Parley P. Pratt, *Autobiography of Parley P. Pratt* (Salt Lake City: Deseret Book, 1985), pp. 260–61.

6. B. H. Roberts, *Life of John Taylor* (Salt Lake City: Bookcraft, 1965), pp. 39–40.

7. Pratt, *Autobiography,* p. 144.

8. David O. McKay, *Cherished Experiences from the Writings of President David O. McKay,* comp. Clare Middlemiss (Salt Lake City: Deseret Book, 1955), pp. 22–24.

9. Brigham Young, in *Journal of Discourses,* 1:93.

10. Howard W. Hunter, "Come to the God of All Truth," *Ensign,* Sept. 1994, p. 72.

11. Bruce R. McConkie, *Mormon Doctrine,* 2d ed. (Salt Lake City: Bookcraft, 1966), p. 285.

12. *Latter-day Saints' Messenger and Advocate* 2 (October 1835): 199.

13. *Messenger and Advocate* 2 (October 1835): 199.

14. Joseph Smith, *History of The Church of Jesus Christ of Latter-day Saints,* 7 vols., 2d ed. rev., ed. B. H. Roberts (Salt Lake City: The Church of Jesus Christ of Latter-day Saints, 1932–51), 4:461.

INDEX